"Forty-two meditations to reset your life! Uprising is an invitation to re-new our mindset in 42 beautiful devotions. Kimber's words are like a tuning fork, showing us aspects where we are flat and out of tune in our thinking. She has a gift to call out our true selves with her words and the truths she speaks—simple truths that change our minds about who we think we are and who we think others are. When our minds can change, our hearts can heal."

Lily Crowder, Author of *Grace for the Contemplative Parent*

"Kimber invites grace, insight and valuable inquiry in this work. I felt challenged, inspired and empowered each day as I meditated on a new entry. It is my belief that we have to feel to heal and in this work Kimber will invite you to feel in all the right ways. Kimber does a stunning job of offering spiritual insight and discovery along with self-acknowledg-ment and understanding. I highly recommend taking time to dive into the self-discovery and inquiry Kimber offers in this book!"

Heather Collins, Yoga Instructor

"What an honor to endorse this amazing book! Turn each page and expe-rience the raw vulnerability of Kimber's journey, while finding yourself amidst her story. Trust the investment you partake in as you see and remember the fully whole person you are created to be."

Dr. Sharnael Wolverton, Swiftfire Ministries International, www.swiftfire.org

"Uprising helped me face my crippling fear and daily dread by unpack-ing my thoughts. Kimber's authentic and raw style encouraged me to see through a new lens of acceptance and positivity—a new sense of self. I highly recommend this book!"

Kim Gibbs, Artist, www.kgfinearts.com

UPRISING:
THE HAPPINESS SHIFT!

Scriptural quotations are taken from a wide variety of translations. Each quotation includes the relevant reference to the translation used.

Order at: Kimberbritner.com and Amazon.com

Kimberbritner@gmail.com

First edition, 2019

www.kimberbritner.com
www.instagram.com/kimberbritnerdesigns
www.facebook.com/kimberbritnerbiz
www.twitter.com/kimberbritner

ISBN: 978-0-9882002-1-0

Cover photograph: Tina Botzenhardt.
Author photo: Gabriel Everett

UPRISING:
THE HAPPINESS SHIFT!

A 40-Day Guide to Shift Out of Fear into Redonkulous Joy

KIMBER BRITNER

CONTENTS

ACKNOWLEDGMENTS

I'm forever grateful to the wild souls, the blazing young hearts, pushing beyond the meals of cardboard, because they know there's more color out there and within themselves than they can even imagine.

Thank you to those bright lights of welcome and bravery that have helped me remember the girl I used to be who danced across Studio 54 and LA clubs with riotously big earrings and fishnet stockings. The girl whose thirst for life pushed me past the limitations of my crazy-train upbringing into creative reframing that's led me home to myself.

To all those badass women in my coaching group who spent six months test-driving this book and walking the road of personal transparency and transformation: I love you!

To those with this book in your hands: The journey of your own uprising and happiness shift awaits you. Dive in!

UPRISING: THE HAPPINESS SHIFT!

INTRODUCTION

I am a content creator. I've created content in the way of books, programs and art since childhood. During the process, there's usually an incubation period while the content ripens and becomes clearer.

As I became intentional about creating new classes for the women I serve, an upsurge of inspiration came forth and was translated into the work I do with others. It was as if a spout in heaven was turned on, pouring new insight into my soul.

The theme of abundance has continued to be highlighted in my life, even though most of our thinking supports the underlying belief that there isn't enough to go around. "Scarcity thinking" can be equated with the lie that the universe is withholding from us. The definition of scarcity thinking is the belief that there just isn't enough to go around!

Starving One's Self

Like many women I know, I had an eating disorder when I was young. I was living in Los Angeles and pursuing an acting career, spinning blindly in place. My disorder began when my world felt out of control, and I discovered that the one thing I could control was my food intake—or lack of it. This gave me a false sense of power and control over my out-of-control world.

Some have said anorexia equates to starving for attention. It's a sentiment with which I might have to agree, because I was starving to be seen and heard and paid attention to—by myself! I had no idea how to truly listen to what my heart was trying to tell me.

When my dear grandmother passed away, I went home to our family farm and suddenly couldn't stop eating the cakes and casseroles the community of supportive friends brought over for us. Within two weeks I had gained twenty pounds, and it was as if a switch had been flipped. All I could think about was planning my next binge. Soon I began binging and purging regularly, desperately attending Overeaters Anonymous meetings and seeing a therapist three times a week.

I compulsively and uncontrollably ate whole boxes of cereal, loaves of bread, jars of peanut butter with honey and sticks of butter, after which I often passed out from the high carbohydrate intake. This plaguing obsession dominated my life for six years.

Then one day, I was miraculously healed. My husband came home from work and discovered me in a heap, crying over two devoured bags of cookies. A pastor friend was summoned and prayed for me during the quiet of a summer evening. With no thunderclap or lightning bolt, all compulsion around food was gone. It was a congenial little prayer that brought with it no evidence that there had been change, but when I had the first bite of "off-limits" food, I was completely satisfied with the appropriate amount. Thirty-plus years later, I am still free from that awful obsession with food.

I remember the first time I was able to eat a handful of potato chips and not the entire bag, or two cookies, rather than two boxes. The freedom was indescribable. Although my relationship to food was instantly altered, some of my thinking remained the same.

I no longer starved or gorged myself with food, but I starved myself in other ways. I had fundamentally pushed back from the table of life without noticing it. It seemed I had rationed and sanctioned the amount of life and enjoyment I deemed permissible. I had, in fact, continued to starve myself through a host of different methods.

When this insight came down the line, I began to recognize its universal posture and nature. The way we handle food—starving, gorging or binging—is merely a reflection of deeper, inner perceptions. Whether in regard to food or emotions, many are withholding and hoarding, fearing that there isn't enough, that they aren't enough, or that the little they have will wither and fly away. We are a people with a scarcity mindset and we don't even know it.

Why Would We Ration Our World?

You may be thinking, "I don't have issues with food." "I don't ration or withhold, binge or gorge." But other areas, ones that you might not expect, can exhibit these patterns too. Let's look at some of those areas and expose scarcity thinking in other forms.

Did you know that fear, something everyone deals with, is the greatest evidence of scarcity thinking in our lives? We have ways of masking it, pulling up our boots and soldiering on, and we have certainly developed clever ways of off-loading and camouflaging it; nevertheless, fear reveals a limited perspective.

Below are some common clues that reveal scarcity, resistance and fear (all of the same coin):

- Excuses and avoidance of something

- Feelings of anxiety or panic

- Blaming

- Being stuck in relationships or cultures that do not resonate with us

- Thinking like a victim

- Wanting to make changes, but being unable to move forward

- Replaying the same story from our life over and over

- Negativity

- Thinking, "I don't have enough," "I am not enough" or "There isn't enough of something out there for me"

"If we've ever experienced any of these manifestations or countless others, we have experienced scarcity, resistance and fear.

I came to the point (or more accurately, the point was revealed to me) where I wanted to surpass my limitations. I wanted to challenge my limiting beliefs so that I would no longer be limited! Limitation is merely a perception, and so I made the bold leap and decided to willingly confront my perceptions.

Anytime we allow our minds to change, we have the potential to realign and receive an upgrade in our thinking that manifests outwardly in our lives. Every outer change is preceded by an inner adjustment. My instantaneous healing with food was a picture of just how fast the shift can occur. I have had others like it.

Now, when I discover an area in my life that is frustrating, painful, causes sadness or despair and is seemingly unchangeable, I determine fear, resistance and the belief in scarcity are hidden beneath my conscious awareness. Nowadays, I get excited when I recognize resistance because I know that I have an amazing opportunity to move past my blocks and receive an upgrade in perspective.

Come along with me as we unwrap resistance, scarcity, ego and fear, and discover the abundance of a brand new way of seeing and thinking and living. Get ready to experience an inner uprising!

PART I:

Joy Doesn't Exist without Self–Permission and Welcome

Most of us fly through life unaware of the previously established settings controlling us. In Part I, we will explore some of the default settings that may be driving the bus. We will explore topics in which you'll identify yourself and nod your head in recognition. For the greatest impact, look beyond the stories that are not your personal experience to uncover your unique defaults standing in the way of your happiness.

WEEK 1:

Why the Resistance?

Day 1: Resistant to Resistance

Day 2: There Is Enough for You

Day 3: You Are Home: Gratitude the Master Shifter

Day 4: No One Can Hold You Back

Day 5: Letting Go

Day 6: Breathe In Nurture

Day 7: Uprising: There Is No Lack or Shortage

INTRODUCTION TO WEEK 1

Why the Resistance?

For years I struggled to get comfortable in the skin of my innate, empathic, spiritual nature. This propensity didn't look like what was modeled in my family, where no one really talked about God or a deep spiritual connection greater than ourselves. Naturally, this made me question my very nature.

As my curiosity to explore the deep mysteries of God and his relationship with humanity increased, I found myself steeped in a spiritual community where I stretched and grew. Ultimately, it wasn't quite the right fit and kept me out of sync with myself for years.

It wasn't until my ability to quietly fit in broke, landing me on the outside looking in, that I recognized that often it's in discovering who we are not that we discover who we truly are. The difficult or awkward seasons can be a tremendous gift, showing us areas of fear, resistance and scarcity within ourselves that keep us from our best.

It took a long time, but I slowly began to recognize the deep patterns of fear and resistance within myself that kept me off-kilter. I began to give myself permission to look, speak, feel and act differently than the crowd and to care for myself in a whole new way.

In Glennon Doyle Melton's truth-telling book, *Love Warrior*, she refers to her own awakening through which she no longer wanted to send in a "representative" to handle life in her place.[1] Instead, she determined to show up in the fullness of who she is. Although this road of living fully may feel far less traveled than the alternative, more of us than you might think are standing at a crossroads, trying to choose which one to follow. We should all choose the path that allows us to show up authentically and nurture our inner world. In the end, that's all that is truly enduring. Choosing this route will require recognizing one's inner resistance and incongruences.

Too Much Adaptability?

Thinking I needed to look like everyone else or care for everyone's discomfort kept me utterly out of touch with my perfectly designed core self. Instead of growing into the unique expression wrapped inside of me, I betrayed my very handcraftedness by trying to imitate already designed prototypes.

Many of us have spent so much time looking outwardly for ourselves and our right fit that we've totally missed the fact that who we are and what we bring is meant to be unique. We're one-of-a-kind. For heaven's sake, there's no other person with the same fingerprint, so why should we try to be like anyone else?

Living outside oneself creates pain and sadness. One of the telltale signs through which I began to recognize that I had shoehorned myself into wrong fits was the lack of joy and happiness in my life. I also recognized this same epidemic in the community of spiritual folks claiming to have the answers.

There seemed to be a malaise that covered our hearing and sight, rendering

---

1   Glennon Doyle Melton, *Love Warrior* (New York: Flat Iron Books, 2016), 132.

us deaf and blind. While our words sounded right, reality betrayed the words. My gut knew that there had to be more freedom than what I was personally experiencing or seeing in others.

This realization inspired me to begin listening to the words I spoke and the messages I said to myself that were false and incongruent with my core. I began to pay attention to my feelings, which for years I had labeled as evil and unreliable. I began to recognize how discombobulated my insides were from denying my resistance and the incongruences within and around me.

Letting go of solidarity with the "right" words and beliefs and instead connecting to the truth of what's really going on within seems an obvious step, yet few are willing to get honest and investigate the truth within themselves. Slowly I began to get comfortable with thinking outside of mimicked and rote answers, even though my lack of parroting made others hugely uncomfortable. I began to find my vein that connected to my core, a resonance that continued to bring peace and fullness of life as I listened and responded to my own invitation to freedom.

I began to nurture the consistent pull toward joy, lightheartedness and hope rather than staying in the struggle of my story, victimhood and powerlessness. I began to awaken and return to the distant song in my heart, foot-tapping and life-releasing. And I consistently chose to give up the lies and beliefs that tethered me to the familiar cul-de-sac of hopelessness and despair.

As I began to experience delight again, I knew I had to nurture and guard the reservoir within myself. Sadly, I discovered that many are not willing to give up their comfortable helplessness and false beliefs, and my choosing to do so posed a threat. When pain and victimhood have kept us company for years, choosing to let go is an absolute act of defiance and realignment of life. It's one of the greatest acts of violence against inner falsehood we can experience, while ushering in the greatest upgrade and uprising imaginable.

Resistance Is a Messenger Worth Befriending

What keeps us from letting go of the wrong fits, dissonance and resistance in our lives, the things that keep us shackled and powerless in victimhood?

Some of us think of resistance as a thing to be bullied and forcefully overtaken. In some sense, that kind of thinking has merit. If something is holding us back, we need to face it rather than coddle it. However, that kind of thinking also has a sense of betrayal attached to it because, after all, there is a person there in this mix of all of the resistance, and that resistance is you and me trying to send a message to command central.

We can listen for the message trying to get through or ignore it and press onward, which usually has conflicting and adverse results. You've probably seen this in your own life.

We don't resist change just for the heck of it. We don't believe the things we believe that keep us covered in fear needlessly. We do these things in an attempt to survive our pain and fear.

Although we might have carefully tucked and stowed away our emotions and other aspects of ourselves, they're still there, lodged somewhere beneath the surface. Wouldn't it be better to befriend these aspects of ourselves and become clear on what they have to reveal to us, rather than betray, compartmentalize and banish them away?

Until we take the time to understand our resistance and actually see it as a friend, we won't be able to receive the messages it's sending, make choices, let go or move beyond it.

DAY 1: RESISTANT TO RESISTANCE

Fear is insidious. It can hide and be camouflaged and diverted in a thousand different ways. One of the most interesting things about fear and its companion, resistance, is our tendency to become resistant to our very resistance. Wow, that's a mind-blower!

You know that feeling of constantly being pulled into the same old vortex of confusion with no clear path out of the dark and back into the light? That could be described as resistance to resistance, or being so afraid and resistant to life that it paralyzes you, so you resist your resistance! Ever been there? I sure have!

Sometimes we are so conditioned by our fears that we refuse to even look at them, having learned to plow through and cope. The feeling fear elicits can be so horrifying that we can't even begin to pull back the covers to peer into reality. Yep, that's resistance to being afraid! Sometimes we're so armored against fear that we don't even know it's there!

All it takes to begin a shift is the littlest step toward willingness. All it takes is acknowledgement. "There's something going on here that I need to look at, even though I don't have a clue what it is! It will not overtake me to just sit, feel, observe and look for clues."

This small bit of willingness will begin to oil the hinges of the ironclad door that we have long kept locked and barred. It will begin to increase awareness.

The willingness to kindly say, "I must be afraid and in some sort of resistance here," is powerful. So today, try this baby step of acknowledgement around an area that has refused to budge in your life. Begin to sit still, peel back the cover and observe.

Perception Challenge and Exercise

Are you willing and open to discovering more? Where do you see immovability in your life and the same old issues that won't budge?

Take some quiet time alone today to journal around this block and the fear connected to it. These first steps can often cause things to come up that you didn't even know were hidden beneath the surface.

Try this: Start writing with an endearing greeting to yourself like "Hello Sweet Pea" or "I see you baby girl! I am eager to hear what you want to say to me" or "Babe, I am all ears! What's going on?"

Now that you've set the tone with a welcome instead of a harsh, condemning environment, you're holding a space of non-judgment for yourself. No one would want to cozy up for a finger-wagging scolding or to receive condemnation and judgment, but often that's the kind of brutality we inflict upon ourselves.

Creating a safe climate of welcome and acceptance elicits willingness to show up true. If you've taken any of my programs, you might know that I have coined the phrase *personal hospitality*. We need constant reminders and practice to hold this hospitable space for ourselves.

As you pause to observe, listen for clues about what fears and resistance are showing up. Listen for ego's posturing to hide and protect you from exposing your very human imperfections. Listen to the ways you want to trail off in dialogue about other people, and remember to stay focused on *you*, your fear and befriending your resistance.

Uprising! New Belief: Today, as you begin, all you need do is choose willingness to rise up beyond where you are to observe and investigate so you can begin to see things from a new perspective.

Repeat out loud: Today, I choose to let go of hiding behind my fear and resistance, and I choose willingness and openness to observe things as they are instead of coping and ignoring them.

Congratulate yourself on practicing the courage to move forward. Freedom and happiness are available and waiting for you. I am cheering you on as you choose willingness to observe and explore the blocks of resistance that have held you back.

DAY 2: THERE IS ENOUGH FOR YOU

My biggest breakthrough around fear and resistance came when I recognized that it always carried the same hidden message lurking beneath the words "There isn't enough _____" or "You aren't enough!"

I began to realize that I had bought into this false belief a long time ago. I had looked around at my situation and determined that I wasn't getting enough. There wasn't enough to go around and there wasn't enough for me.

This perception of lack came with me into adulthood and seeped into every corner of my life. There was no way to have this fundamental belief in one area and not have it carry through into other areas. It was the lens through which I saw the world, made decisions, monitored my wants and desires and ultimately limited myself, without ever recognizing it!

Mind you, this common perspective actually has nothing to do with whether or not there is a lack or insufficiency in our lives. We are humans living in a very human world, so there will always be messages of insufficiency and lack from all sides, but choosing to see the world from the lens of fullness or absence is absolutely a personal decision. I imagine that this is a big nugget for you to chew on right now, with your particular story countering and trailing beside you.

Imagine what would have happened if, while experiencing actual lack or the perception of it as a child, I chose to see fullness. If I'd chosen to see fullness, the lack that I perceived would have suddenly become a reality of ample provision and abundance though my young eyes.

There is a famous Ronald Reagan analogy that has stuck with me about a boy in a stall full of manure, declaring, "There must be a pony in here somewhere!" Now, *that's* the kind of expansive possibility and abundant thinking that I want to possess.

The world will quickly try to discourage this kind of optimism with terms like "realist" and "facts," but those who refuse to let their possibility lenses be diminished are the happiest folks in the world. They see the world as fully supplied rather than bitter, stingy and dying. It's easy to find the dirt. Let's be the ones to find the gold.

That is the way I intend to be and see the world. Every time I bump up against the ugly scarcity lens of bitterness, fearfulness and discouragement in others or myself, I want to stay true to joy and the belief in more. While writing this I can feel the fire of truth lighting my spirit, and that is what I've learned to lean into. The cold water of fear will douse faith every time. When we lean into the light of hope, faith and joy, we become an accelerant to the flame!

One of the ways we can do this is by learning to establish boundaries in our lives and our relationships. For years I let groupthink trample my own good opinion and discernment, because I had no boundaries in place. In an attempt to exercise kindness and compassion, I failed to give them to myself. It is a fallacy to think we can give to others what we've failed to give ourselves.

Perception Challenge and Exercise

Willingness to see differently begins with a decision, not a circumstantial change. It doesn't mean you have all the answers; it means you're not willing to settle for the old, comfortable ways of coping that have knowingly or unknowingly been shutting you down or killing you bit by bit.

Sometimes negativity is so ingrained in us that we have to be reminded of what it feels like to believe, to have faith that there is enough and that we are enough. It's often our false perceptions and fears that scare us into limitations and trigger us to shut down our feelings. However, feelings aren't the issue; it's willingness to address them and determine the truth about them. It's taking ownership of whether a feeling will control us or we will control how we choose to see and feel.

Did you know that leaning into life-giving feelings or energy has the power to shift your energy? Remember a time, maybe when you were young or maybe yesterday, when you felt elated, hopeful and full of joy. Now, stir up that memory.

Feel what it felt like to have joy rumbling inside you and lean into it. Let your body and brain feel the refreshing wave wash over you like a river spring. Dip your toes into the joy, and now slide all the way in. Nurture this feeling and open posture, as if you were a child running into a waterfall. Nurture this wide-open spaciousness and don't let it be stolen. If you surrender it, you can always capture it again because it is within you!

This will be more difficult for some than others because skepticism has built up within their hearts. You can bring the walls down with consistent attention and willingness to take a dip in refreshing springs instead of stagnant water.

Picture yourself receiving new gifts of every kind: friendship, opportunities, finances, provision and nurturance. Imagine this unlimited supply of provision and internal wholeness as a reality coming to you through a power greater than yourself, through God. There is enough! You merely have to be willing to receive it and give up your attachment to scarcity and limitation. The first boundary you may need to establish is with your own negativity.

Uprising! New Belief: This is where you get to decide to throw out the old, limiting beliefs that "there isn't enough for you" and that "you are not enough" and choose to believe that there is an abundant supply in the universe and it is for you! However, you might not be clear about what limiting beliefs are hindering you and keeping you "not enoughing," so I suggest you throw it out to God and the universe and ask that your particular limiting beliefs be made clear to you. Ask to see where you're getting tripped up.

This is where working one-on-one with a life coach is invaluable. A good coach will immediately hear the limiting beliefs you're communicating and help lead you into freedom.

Repeat out loud: Today I choose to believe that there is enough for me in this abundant universe. I choose to release my old ideas of limitation and become open, and to expand my perceptions and beliefs around abundance. I am willing to establish healthy boundaries in my life to facilitate caring for myself.

DAY 3: YOU ARE HOME: GRATITUDE THE MASTER SHIFTER

Part of a scarcity mindset is the feeling that we're always searching for home but it's nowhere to be found. Some say this is because we are passing through and this isn't our permanent home. I believe that's a convenient excuse to stay in the struggle and discontentedness when we fail to recognize home within ourselves.

You already know I believed for a large portion of my life that there wasn't enough for me. This carried over into feeling like an orphan. My sister and I actually laughed about feeling this way when we weren't crying. Sadly, I attached to what some have called an "orphan spirit," or the feeling of being orphaned. How do you think that served me?

Whether we're literal orphans or people who didn't receive healthy nurturing and parenting, there is higher parenting that we need to recognize. I too had to recognize this reality for myself. This is not to deny what we may have experienced, but rather it is the intentional choice to move beyond the pain of what's limiting us today.

Once, I participated in a creative collage workshop with maps. The instructor incorporated questions like "Where am I?" "Where is home?" and "Will I ever arrive?" As I contemplated my piece, I heard within my spirit, "You are already home, because home is within you."

I immediately knew this message was addressing the limiting belief I had regarding feeling orphaned and homeless. Suddenly a sense of peace flooded my being as this new truth settled me into home. I no longer search for something elusive because I carry home with me. Interestingly, shortly after this internal shift transpired, an outer shift manifested and we purchased a home.

Grieving Losses

Before I began to recognize the lie I'd believed, there was a sense of grieving the wasted time and pain I'd caused myself. Sometimes we need to grieve our losses, but we also need to recognize that we did the best we could with the resources we had at the time. We don't have to linger and bemoan what was when we have the opportunity to choose a new perspective now!

Nevertheless, I want to point out that I'm not against grieving. Grief is real and needs to be felt, rather than suppressed, especially when we lose important people in our lives or go through trauma or difficult transitions. Grief is a natural expression of loss.

There is no one-size-fits-all grieving formula. Having experienced a significant amount of loss in my life, I can tell you that how I grieved looked different each time. When my sister and I lost our mom, how we grieved looked very different from and in some respects was the exact opposite of what I would have expected.

The only way to truly process grief is to give ourselves time and permission to do so. The end! As time goes on, we usually find the urge to embrace life. Learning grows and grief diminishes.

When we shift our focus from what we've lost or don't have into gratitude for the abundance that we do have, significant shifts happen. And they happen like a ripple effect, all through our life. Gratitude is the ultimate perspective shifter and upgrade giver! It is key to rising up and key to our uprising!

Perception Challenge and Exercise

Choosing to let go of long-held beliefs can come instantly or with a struggle. You can cling to the struggle as much as you want, or you can let go and enter into home, beautifully tailored to fit you.

Do you feel like you lack "home?" Today, define for yourself your own sense of home and what those characteristics of home look like to you.

Example: To me, home is a place where I can show up as I am. It's a deeply spiritual place of quiet listening and welcoming each part of myself. Home is a place where I am surrounded by beauty internally and externally. Home is an environment of hospitality, generosity, laughter and creativity, in which friends and family gather to play in my studio, or under the stars at night for a luscious backyard BBQ with specialty cocktails and twinkly lights.

This may express external images, but it also creatively expresses the flavor of my inner being. Describe your sense of home.

Uprising! New Belief: You are as much at home as you choose to be. An orphan identity need not follow you or define you any longer than you allow it. You carry home with you, so why wouldn't it reflect the truest part of you and your Maker? You are a beautiful, exquisite habitat and sanctuary, and to think of yourself as anything less reveals a scarcity mindset. Enlarge your perspective. Become the home you've always wanted to be.

Repeat out loud: I've been unkind to myself in my refusal to welcome all parts of me home. I've often judged and held acceptance at a distance, although I am the greatest place of welcome and hospitality that exists for myself. Today, I start rolling out the welcome mat. I am settling in and recognizing the tremendous shelter, habitat and sanctuary that I am because of the Godly nature that I possess. I open myself up to a new spiritual dynamic that I may not have recognized before. I am the house of God.

home - Security, Safety, love, warmth
a place where no one can hurt you
a place of self healing
a place of love in abudance
a Place of forgivness
a Place of warm memories
a Place of trust

DAY 4: NO ONE CAN HOLD YOU BACK

Our stories are unique and beautiful and can be inspiring when they cease tying us down and having power over us. Honestly, some of us are not quite ready to give up our stories. We're not ready to love what is.

When we have a list of "buts" standing in our way, it's hard to love what is.

When ego is fighting to win or be vindicated for our pain, it's hard to settle into and accept what is. The hard truth is that for our stories to cease controlling us, we have to let go of our addiction to suffering and limitation and adamantly reject ego's favorite role of martyr and victim. We will discuss this in greater depth as we move forward, but for today, chew on this rich piece of meat and enjoy this fun little slice of wisdom below.

In *Big Magic*, Elizabeth Gilbert gives us a lively picture of the roles of the Martyr and the Trickster. I believe the inspiration of the Trickster can pull us out of being trapped beneath our story, if we're willing to see it.

> Martyr says: "I will sacrifice everything to fight this unwinnable war, even if it means being crushed to death under a wheel of torment."
>
> Trickster says: "Okay, you enjoy that! As for me, I'll be over here in this corner, running a successful little black market operation on the side of your unwinnable war."
>
> Martyr says: "Life is pain."
>
> Trickster says: "Life is interesting."[2]

Elizabeth Gilbert, *Big Magic* (New York: Penguin Random House, Riverhead Books, 2015), 222.

When we live from the place of Martyr, aching to be seen for the heroics of our suffering, the only one clamoring to see, hear and acknowledge our pain is ourself! We're waiting for us to show up for ourself and not anyone else. But until we do, we will continue looking off into the distance for someone to validate and acknowledge our story. All the while, we're the only one who can honestly give us what we need. We can't get it from outside ourself. And so, we get to decide: Trickster or Martyr? Easy or hard?

Perception Challenge and Exercise

How willing are you to let go of your pain and victimhood in exchange for freedom and happiness? That means letting go of your story and of playing the starring victim and martyr in it.

For a moment, set aside the tendency toward victimhood that you may have and try on the Trickster. The creative brainstormer, shape-shifter, dream-believer that resides inside of you may have been squashed because it can only survive and thrive in the freedom of wide-open territory. You can always call her back anytime you choose and exchange your pain for innovation.

Reclaim the wide-eyed big thinker that as a child ruled the roost in you and let her free. Redefine yourself as trickster, dreamer, innovator—you name it!

Uprising! New Belief: As we gradually dive into perception shifts and learn how to fuel them, I hope you're getting excited about the actual power you possess to direct your life. In doing so, you can connect to your own abundant source of Big Magic. That certainly will result in a gargantuan upgrade and a huge shift in happiness.

Repeat out loud: I deserve a full and happy life and, to that end, I choose to happily abandon my need to be the victim or martyr in my story. I choose to redefine the starring role I live. In fact, I choose carefree, fun, adventurous, fully supplied and supported, innovative genius!

DAY 5: LETTING GO

I've spent various seasons of my life working through hurdles and choosing willingness to forgive offenses when I didn't want to or know how to. Yet I never imagined that the work I would need to do the most was to forgive myself.

Revisiting this topic reminds me of my heartbreaking self-betrayal. Without acknowledging where I've been, I am not free to make the choice to leave it behind.

Here are ten areas where I've had to grant myself forgiveness:

- Being a hard-driving taskmaster with my
  tender, young heart.

- Over-adulting and imposing too great a burden
  of responsibility on my carefree, young self.

- Throwing the Madonna-singing, fishnet-wearing and
  bikini-toting fun girl I once was to the wolves of propriety
  and rigidity.

- Failing to protect my kids from abusive religion.

- Not being brave enough to hear my heart saying,
  "No, that's not who I am."

- Prostituting myself in different ways until I lost my song.

- Betraying my deeply spiritual self in order to line
  up and look normal.

- Almost killing the passionate girl I was through performance and efficiency.

- Not knowing how to love myself and making myself scrounge for love.

- Striving for perfection and burying my deeply feeling heart.

If I hadn't recognized the ways I pushed and prodded myself into subservient behavior, I wouldn't have given myself permission to find a better way.

It's interesting that few of us recognize the hard-driving way we've "managed" ourselves because it's been our normal. There is nothing more liberating than letting go of what isn't working, ceasing to feed oneself poison and learning to nourish oneself with love and goodness. Welcome to the happy reality of letting go!

Perception Challenge and Exercise

Maybe you didn't struggle with compliance, but rebelled. If you stop to listen to your heart, you too will most likely find ways you betrayed your heart's needs. And you too can give yourself the gift of self-forgiveness.

What is that thing tugging at you for which you need to forgive yourself? How have you been holding yourself hostage? Spend some time writing out all of the wrongs you need to right with yourself, because girlfriend, it's your release date! It's time to set yourself free. It's time for granting self-forgiveness.

Uprising! New Belief: I'm pretty sure that if your precious baby girl did something that hurt you, you would choose to forgive her. I am pretty sure you wouldn't be able to help yourself. Why would you hold yourself in any less regard? There's no reason to hold any past offense over your own head. All you have to do is let go and walk away free. Baby girl, let yourself free!

Repeat out loud: I release myself from any self-hatred and judgment I've held over myself. It is time to let it go. I forgive myself for _____, once and for all! It's finished! I receive love for myself, now.

- Sometimes loss of Self-control
- feelings of hurt and letting it rule me
- giving up when things get too hard
- Selfishness — making up for lack of Self-love.

DAY 6: BREATHE IN NURTURE

Sometimes I think we navigate through life with our breath held. When I'm focusing intently on an action such as trying to open a tight jar lid, I sometimes find myself sighing because I've been holding my breath.

Breathing is natural and automatic, and yet most of us give very little thought to the wonder of it. If we're starving our being of the nurturance, attention, kindness and actual air supply it needs, imagine the message we're sending to ourselves.

Pilates, yoga and breath work classes all focus on the breath. Spending an entire hour breathing deeply while practicing yoga or attending a breath work class is exhilarating. Some people experience a release of pent-up emotion and cry, while others laugh. With all that fresh oxygen pumping through the lungs, we can't help but experience a total-body exhilaration tingling from our head to our toes. It's a powerfully cleansing experience that I highly recommend.

Nature is the all-time equalizer. Stepping outside to breathe in the beauty around us or pausing to realign with the majesty of our beautifully crafted bodies helps us realign and connect with the bigger picture in life, which is our Source and Love supply. On day six of each week, we will focus on the idea of our breath and breathing in important aspects of life and connection to our Source.

At times, we falsely believe we are disconnected from God, Source or Spirit because of distractions and busyness. However, separation is not possible, but only an illusion.

Nature has a grounding effect that helps us recognize God's omnipresence, making us aware that all of life is sacred whether in a trash heap or a cathedral. All we need do is see beyond our circumstances. Often we fail to recognize this and are whisked away into mental illusions of our own making.

Perception Challenge and Exercise

Do you find yourself hunkering down in difficult situations and forgetting to breathe? Today, slow down and become aware of your breath. Take in big, full breaths and breathe out loud, deep sighs. With each breath, feel the God life in you, powering your body and your lungs. Connect to your breath and connect to the Source within you.

Whether you allow for time to take a long walk, soaking in the beauty of nature around you, or to view the big blue sky on your drive into work, place your awareness on the vastness of the air supporting you, around you and through you. Let your breath fill up every part of your being.

Uprising! New Belief: Recognize that you are not merely floating through this world alone, but you are eternally connected to Love and its life force. You are surrounded by Love and any feeling of separation and disconnection is merely an illusion. At any time, you can refocus your gaze on Love and realign your awareness to your connection.

Repeat out loud: I am fully supplied with this magnificent, sustaining breath that feeds life to every part of my being. I will practice holding awareness around the oxygen I breathe, recognizing that Love is filling up my lungs. With each breath, I am being fully supported and connected to Love.

DAY 7: UPRISING: THERE IS NO LACK OR SHORTAGE

We like to believe that our situation is blocking us. All the while, we never stop to consider that our perception or resistance is blocking us and keeping us in a reality that looks and feels exactly like limitation. Resistance and fear hinder our sight and always keep us living below what is actually available for us. Limitation is merely a perception.

Since childhood I've been an empathic girl who deeply senses things; I've always seen pictures in the spiritual realm and received information I couldn't possibly have known. There have been plenty of times that I haven't understood what I was seeing or sensing. Sometimes it's been years before things have become clear, as in the hordes of people fleeing from 9/11's burning towers that I saw years prior to the event. And there are things I will certainly never understand.

It took me a long time to recognize this as my normal and my children's normal too. Some people have terms for this like Seer, Mystic, Empath and Prophet, but I shy away from definitions. I wrote a song when I was sixteen entitled "Life Doesn't Come with Instructions," and I would say this tendency doesn't either.

I consider this sensibility a form of spiritual guidance and a gift from God that helps me learn more about God and myself so I can better navigate life and support those around me. The more I tune into this intuitive part of my nature, the more expansiveness I find in experiencing life. The more I deny and try to bury this part of myself, the more resistance and limitation I create for myself.

I'm not so different from anyone else. I believe we all have this same capability. It's merely whether or not we learn to grow our sensitivity to it.

Wide-Angle Vision

There have been times when strangers recognized this sensibility within our family and spoke about it to us. Some things I dismissed long ago because I didn't understand them. More than once someone told me they saw me on the red carpet.

When I was young, having had an impotent career in Hollywood and no longer being interested in such notoriety, I dismissed this as something someone picked up on from my past. It wasn't until I began to recognize the vast limitation and scarcity mindset I had subjected myself to that I began to view the red carpet as an upgrade in an abundance perspective.

Once, this wide-angle perspective was spoken over my eldest son, Gabriel. A person told him they saw him going up in an elevator high above the city so that he could see and discern what was going on at a higher level.

Another time, I had a unique encounter or vision in which I saw the most beautiful home and I knew I was being asked what I wanted, implying that I could have anything. Not knowing what to make of the invitation, my suspicious mind wondered if it was a trick question. Some time later, I realized the conversation wasn't a special promise that I could request a yacht or Bentley and boom it would appear like a genie granting me three wishes. It was a deeper look into what I actually believed and perceived as possible.

We can stay in limitation as long as our little hearts desire, or we can have the faith to believe in a limitless God that surpasses anything we might think or understand. This doesn't mean reducing God to Santa Claus. However, I believe Love is far more generous than we have dared to imagine.

These encounters speak to me of what is available to all of us. If we're willing to challenge our resistance, fear and ideas of limitation, we might discover unlimited abundance and resources. A person who chooses to see and experience an oasis in the desert is rich.

Now, I understand that this kind of conversation in and of itself can be a challenge. It's mysterious, uncertain and vague, to say the least. If I am honest, there are days when I am covered in fear and can't see my way out of a paper bag, much less have faith for limitlessness or navigating the supernatural. Nevertheless, I fundamentally believe that with a limitless universe there is no limit to how far Love can take us if we aren't standing in our own way.

God Perspectives

I believe that limitation ultimately comes down to our perception of God. Why would I say that? If we believe in a being that is all-powerful, that being will not be hindered by limitation or short supply.

If God and the universe are limitless, every time we find ourselves casting limitation on a situation and doubting possibility, it is not because of the failure of an all-powerful being, but because of our own perceptions and lack of faith.

WEEK 1

Good God or Bad God?

We might blame the shortage that we see in the world on God, but is it really God's fault? Is hunger in the world due to a stingy God, or is it because we live in a society that allows for lack and fails to care for those beyond ourselves? The more my core beliefs center around scarcity, the more I attract it.

Every time we decide our husband is the problem, or that our employer, the facilitator, the relationship, or the people are the problem (been there, done that!), we're in a place of limitation, believing that our supply cannot come because of the person or situation in front of us. Guess what? That's an illusion we're harboring. Where we place the power is where our focus lies. What and where we give our power becomes our god.

Perception Challenge and Exercise

This week has introduced a huge mindset challenge. It may take some time for it to begin to sink in. Here is an opportunity for an upgrade like no other. As long as you support the space in your life for limitation, it will manifest! Challenge yourself regularly to ask the question: Am I giving scarcity and limitation my power, or faith and provision through an abundant, loving God?

Often we think of God in terms of things we do, rather than our connection through relationship. Relationship is the vehicle through which we engage with God. Earlier I wrote about some of my encounters with God that were precipitated through conversation and relationship with God.

As we close this week, spend some time journaling about the areas of your life where you see lack and limitation showing up. Try engaging in conversation with God. Maybe the lack you're experiencing in your life is the nonexistent love relationship you desire. Maybe it's the lack of true camaraderie and friendship. Maybe limitation and scarcity are showing up in your life through financial struggles, an ill-fitting job, a health crisis or general dissatisfaction and unhappiness. Inviting Spirit as your guide, challenge yourself to look beyond the surface to recognize how your thoughts and belief structures are holding you back.

Uprising! New Belief: When you own that you are most likely the source of your unhappiness instead of blaming circumstance or people, you take back your power to change. In truth, you are the one in charge of your happiness. Wherever you feel happiness is lacking in your life, there is a direct correlation to your thoughts and what you believe to be true.

It's time to challenge what you've believed and choose an upgrade out of misery into the joy and happiness that is available if you are willing to change your mind!

Repeat out loud: I choose to change my mind about the way I've seen the world. I choose to let go of my dingy lens of limitation and lack. There has always been ample supply for me, even when I've failed to recognize it. I choose to embrace faith in a fully loving and supplying God and a universe that is good, generous and supportive of me.

WEEK 2:

Love Makes You At Home in Your Own Skin

Day 8: Ego's Song and Dance

Day 9: Free to Have Enough

Day 10: Seeing Abundance

Day 11: "But…" Illusion Debunking

Day 12: Do Yourself a Favor and Let It Go

Day 13: Breathe In Personal Hospitality and Kindness

Day 14: Uprising: Daddy Goodness

INTRODUCTION TO WEEK 2

Love Makes You At Home in Your Own Skin

Last week I talked about the separation illusion I nursed for most of my life, feeling orphaned, unloved and abandoned. When I began to awaken to the reality that I had always been fully loved and cared for, my life began to change dramatically.

Most of us are pretty freewheeling with the word *love*. We use the same word to describe our feelings of loving our new shoes, ice cream and those dearest to us, but we never stop to consider the real character and nature of the word. It's interesting to investigate our real perceptions around love. Do we believe love is fleeting, faulty and human, or merely nostalgic?

When we've attached pain and loss to love, we believe love hurts. When we've attached lust to love, we believe love is merely sexual. When we've had little daddying, it's hard to comprehend a supernatural Love from a good God and Father. We think of love as a thing off in the distance that's hard to obtain, rather than experienced through relationship.

Most of us have measured the reality of love by our circumstances. When we brush up against difficulty, ugliness and pain, we judge the reality of love. However, when we get outside our own experiences and definitions, we might realize that love is far more expansive than our comprehension. While our love may be faulty, divine Love is not flimflam, withholding or based on what we currently feel.

When we hold the space open to look beyond our circumstances and perceptions, the truly unlimited parameters of divine Love begin to waft through our open door to illuminate our awareness. Willingness creates a powerful entry for reception.

Hidden in Plain Sight

It's taken me a lifetime to *begin* to comprehend the expansiveness of a Love that is far beyond human experience or understanding. I can only begin to grasp the tiniest measure of the fullness of Love when I am open to experiencing it through my spirit's inner knowing, rather than the blocks produced by my logical mind. Nevertheless, it's a mystery hidden in plain sight.

The evidence of this Love is far more present than I am aware of and more real than I am capable of understanding. Love's opulent, benevolent, unconditional generosity appears in my life without my "good-girling," trying to measure up and please. It merely is, always has been and always will be. The ultimate opportunity and challenge is to recognize it.

Happiness is not a thing to possess, but an experience of divine Love through relationship. The more willing I am to dance with this mystery, the more happiness unfolds before me. The more I resist a relationship with Love and focus on the illusion that outer things will bring me happiness, the more I find myself in struggle.

I choose to fully believe in the goodness of this unexplainable, majestic Love while continuing to discover its unlimited borders. I find it hard to comprehend those that deny the presence of God's love when they witness the birth of a child or look at the extraordinary examples in nature that mirror the unending cycle of Love surrounding us.

There is no route to real happiness apart from a spiritual journey into Love. This week we will continue to build upon last week's topics regarding the beliefs that hinder us from experiencing the depths of Love that we truly desire.

As we progress, you may notice that the discussion spirals, wrapping around, deepening and reappearing, as I continue to present various facets of the same topics. This is because many of the things we're discussing are intangibles. Happiness is not a thing but a steady unfolding of relationship with Love, one another and primarily ourselves. It's an expanding perception that calls us to awaken to our inner being and our internal reality. Enjoy the ever-winding and unfolding journey.

DAY 8: EGO'S SONG AND DANCE

I don't think I began to understand ego until I saw its connection to fear and resistance in my life. Clarity surfaced as I recognized fearful choices I'd made that created resistance and blockages in my life, all of which were powered by my ego.

Most of us probably don't remember our first experience with shame and humiliation or the response they elicited. I personally don't remember a specific experience, but I do remember feelings of shame and humiliation as a child that made me want to hide. Although humiliation is the sense of embarrassment that comes from feeling exposed, shame is a more intense feeling that carries the message that there is something intrinsically wrong with us. It's this feeling that tells us love has left the building and left us out.

As youngsters we have no understanding that our experiences don't actually define who we are. We are not, in fact, the totality of those terrible, shame-induced feelings. We aren't bad or stupid, silly or unlovable. We aren't the reflection of others' projections onto us. Nevertheless, in our struggle to survive the pain we've felt, ego offers up tricky methods for survival that we all adapt to our lives in some form or another.

Lacking actual tools to navigate emotion and attempting to grapple with feeling unloved and "not enough," ego offers tactics that cause us to shut down and hide, or conversely to become louder and bigger to compensate for feelings of being reduced. Sometimes we alternate between the two, as ego presents different tactics of survival for each of us.

Because the role of parental oversight in my family was unoccupied, my role became that of the hero. I sought to caretake and solve the world's problems. In taking up my cape and boots, I attempted to outrun my pain and *earn* love. Playing the hero also served as a dandy method for hiding my true feelings.

It isn't hard to spot the over-functioners who are working hard with our capes in tow because the rest of the world won't get with the program and help out. For all our martyrdom and grandstanding, we usually receive accolades of praise and validation for being so competent. Though we often fail to see it, workaholism, striving and performing reveal many a person's lack of personal identity and worth.

For years, this tactic worked well to bury my pain. It wasn't until life events exhausted my ability to cope that all my stockpiled pain and emotion began popping up to the surface like bobbers that had broken free.

A Divine Setup

Suddenly the song and dance stopped working and I was caught in the vortex of the in-between, not knowing what to do with the onslaught of emotion I felt. Coincidentally, that's the perfect time to give way and let it all fall apart while choosing to feel all that's been sidelined and shut off for so long.

It's actually a divine setup when our tactics to cover unease and pain stop working. The rub is that because ego doesn't sit with emotion, but consistently throws up shields of masking and avoidance, we must intentionally look deeper. We must allow ourselves to listen to and uncover the ignored messages and emotions within ourselves. Despite our reluctance or cultural refusal to acknowledge feelings, once we intentionally choose to sit with them, we discover that they will not destroy us.

As I did this, I was introduced to a deeper listening within myself than I had ever been willing to sit with before, although I had performed spiritual activities for years. With Spirit's guidance, I began to navigate the landmines of my emotion and ushered in a beautiful discovery of personal care and kindness.

The great paradox is that denial, avoidance and attempting to bury parts of ourselves will only postpone the pain of our self-betrayal and self-rejection, not delete it. Look around and you'll see every sort of failed coping mechanism, be it fixing and caretaking, perfectionism, workaholism, drug abuse, alcoholism, sexual addiction, religious addiction, overeating, shopping, TV or one of many commonly accepted methods.

Remember, most of us have been reliant on ego's coping methods because we've been paralyzed by shame. Shame causes us to believe in the illusion that we are disconnected, adrift and separated from Love, alone and often rejected or abandoned. This sense of separation can feel gaping when viewed through the lens of our unique stories that keep us disassociated from the fully loved truth of ourselves. And sadly, it can occur at any time.

Nevertheless, being created in the image of God means it's impossible to be separated from Love and, equally so, it's impossible to be separated from our spiritual self, although we can be oblivious to it. Once we recognize the illusion that shame and ego have cast upon the screen of our lives, we can begin to awaken and settle into the truth of having always been fully loved. Similarly, when we recognize that fear is born of separation, we can return to the source of Love.

Perception Challenge and Exercise

Maybe you weren't the hero but the helpless one that the hero worked to protect, or maybe you took on another projection entirely that helped you cope. No coping mechanism is more holy or evil than the next; they all cast a false perception of separation from who we truly are. Once we are willing to recognize these false self-projections and let go of the judgment about our song and dance, we can shift into an unlimited view of the world and ourselves. Take stock through the resistance exercise below.

Fear is the same thing as resistance, and it shows up in all the hard, stuck places in our lives. Once we begin to observe our lives, we can begin to identify areas of resistance. When we want change, yet find circumstances immovable, there is usually resistance lurking beneath the surface. Even when we believe the problem or holdup exists outside ourselves, circumstances will not change until we address the resistance within ourselves.

Observing Resistance

Start to observe your resistance. What are the common thoughts that keep you focusing outward instead of recognizing your own inner fear and resistance?

1. Observe and acknowledge when you feel a thought arise that says you're being misunderstood or going unheard. Begin to practice giving yourself the attention you crave rather than looking for it outwardly. Instead of focusing on the lack you perceive from others, begin to recognize the abundance of being present for yourself.

2. Rather than resenting others that aren't responding in a way you'd like, observe where you may be exhibiting the same pattern with yourself and toward others. Practice shifting into positivity instead of negative emotion. Practice giving yourself the welcome and acceptance you crave from others.

3. A sense of abandonment, rejection and lack of belonging reveal fear. The presence of fear is a signal that you're relying on your own strength rather than trusting in the ample provisions available to you. When you feel you're unsupported, recognize that the universe has fully supported and supplied you. Focus on the love surrounding you, rather than the lack you've perceived.

Recognizing resistance and fear in your life opens the way to release it and shift into faith and trust. Observing what you're feeling without judgment helps open the way to shift out of negative energy into the abundance that is already yours. It all begins with a willingness to get curious and observe.

Uprising! New Belief: It is unbelievably liberating to get honest with ourselves and let ourselves off the hook. When I began to recognize that my rescuing coping mechanism was fear-induced and creating resistance in my life while enabling others to remain helpless, I began to be able to let go of the rope. I discovered the world would go on just fine without my over-adulting and I could happily retire!

This caused things to shift around me. I stopped getting accolades for being the highest jumper, but as I grew in personal respect and care for myself, I stopped needing that unreliable approval from others. I began to truly love and respect myself, knowing that I was already fully loved.

Interestingly, my vacated hero spot was quickly filled because when you make a shift, others needing the same validation will sniff out the empty spot and run to grab it. This is true relationally, professionally and even in spiritual climates.

Just so you realize, choosing to intentionally sit out from ego's dog and pony show is entirely different from hiding out because of shame. Hiding out from shame is oppressive and life altering. Hanging up ego's lies and routine to sit with your own self-acceptance and self-respect is empowering. This is a huge upgrade toward happiness and your personal uprising. And although ego will continue to pop its head up, I know you're ready to begin to address your ego-driven tactics and the growing reality of your fully loved identity.

Repeat out loud: It's liberating to get honest with myself about the ways ego has led me down darkened alleys of performance and self-degradation. I no longer have to believe the same lies I've believed about myself. I no longer have to hustle for my own self-respect. I am willing to sit, listen and value myself without striving. I am willing to step into the light of self-love and out of forced labor! I know that I've always been fully loved by God and always will be!

DAY 9: FREE TO HAVE ENOUGH

Because of our perceptions, which are actually beliefs about the world and ourselves, few of us have considered that the way we see the world and live are merely the tracks that our stories created and our perceptions run upon.

When we stop to really let this sink in, it is both sobering and empowering. This means that we are no longer victims to our particular propensities or track. This means that we can redirect the traffic of our lives by altering our perceptions.

I don't know about you, but I am sick and tired of the scarcity, of determining there isn't enough for me before I even get out of bed in the morning. I'm tired of my faithless accusations accusing God of child abuse for what I've perceived as unfairly handling my life or the world.

You might not have considered that your thoughts carry this vein, but ultimately everything leads back to our view of God and the connection of everything and everyone to each other. So if we've believed that there is a shortage of Love for us, we need to take a closer look. We will be talking about this further in Day 14.

Sometimes we can't see the world correctly because we're focused in too tightly on a problem. We can't see the forest for the trees. Is it any wonder that with a limited perspective, many of us are discouraged, depressed, paralyzed and lack the passion to move forward in life?

As a young widow, I began to shift my grief and hopelessness to a wider lens of belief. One day, after a frivolous spin through a fashion magazine, it was as if the captions started to jump off the page and right into my spirit. "It's time to live again! Take hold of your holster, honey, there's no such thing as failure."

I cut out the phrases, pasted them on paper and hung them on my bathroom mirror. And although I had no idea of the effect of this exercise, I soon saw my frightened and overwhelmed heart begin to reboot.

As I fed myself with a new diet of hope and encouragement, I grew in strength and fortitude, and my lifelessness turned into vision for a new future. It all began as I determined to lean into the truth that Love's nature was abundant and never withholding. I chose to see the good instead of dwelling on the bad, to believe there was enough for me and that I was free to have it all!

When we see the world through limitation, it's no wonder we end up on dead-end streets without solutions or provision. However, abundance is a wide-angle vantage point, a bigger picture in which we see the world through the expansive lens of faith.

God is Love, and love's nature is abundant and never withholding. To align with this truth is to consistently shift our thinking, which ultimately shifts everything about our lives.

Perception Challenge and Exercise

Sometimes the tracks you're living on limit you in ways you don't realize. Today, take a good look at the track your life is running on and determine where your beliefs might be limiting you.

Do you consistently bump against familiar patterns of "not enough" and scarcity thinking? Does a love relationship seem out of reach, are true friends impossible to find, or do career opportunities regularly fall through? Write about your discoveries, your accusations toward God or the universe, and explore where a deep-seated belief that there isn't enough could be hindering you.

Then make a gratitude list of all that has been beautifully served up in your life. Maybe the postman smiled and greeted you today. Maybe the sun came out instead of the rain, or maybe the rain came out and watered your garden. But mostly, recognize that today you got to wake up and breathe in one more amazing day of your life! You are loved through and through. Abundance is waiting for you to recognize it.

Take note of any tone you hear cycling around in your thoughts that says, "This happened to me," or "This is happening to me." This tone reveals a victim posture. Where there's a victim posture, there is fear that you are being left out and that there isn't enough for you. That's a very disempowering belief, isn't it?

The truth is that you can choose your posture. You can decide to live from a different energy, something we'll talk about further in the coming days. You can choose to believe that you're supported, rather than forgotten. You can recognize that nothing is withholding joy from you but yourself, no matter your circumstances. Imagine if you refused to feel rejected, slighted, overlooked or unseen, because you were confident in being fully loved.

Uprising! New Belief: Because you've sometimes believed that there isn't enough, it may seem impossible that a shift could easily take place through simply changing your mind. You may believe that change amounts to impossible odds, or an unreasonable amount of heavy lifting or Mount-Everest-climbing.

What if change begins with a realignment of trust? Imagine surrendering blame shifting and accusation of child abuse or unfairness and realigning the negative Eeyore stance of, "For some reason I'm always getting forgotten." Ugh, that's an off-putting posture that I've been guilty of too. Today, you can choose to give up that mistaken tone of distrust and despair!

Repeat out loud: I choose to align and reposition myself into a childlike stance of openness, giving up my unwarranted suspicions concerning God and the universe's faithfulness. Today, I choose to awaken to all that's been gifted to me, believing that I am free to have all of the love I can receive.

DAY 10: SEEING ABUNDANCE

I often talk about the 1960 Disney version of Eleanor Porter's children's classic *Pollyanna*, which tells the tale of a young orphan whose optimistic take on life consists of finding something to be glad about in every situation. By creating the Glad Game, Pollyanna ultimately shifts her whole town's downcast and embittered perspectives and, through an aperture correction, overcomes her own challenges too.

There will always be situations threatening to dim our light. When these situations arrive, there are two options: fear or faith. I remember the day we got the news that my sweet husband, Bill, had stage four brain cancer. That night, as I sat in the bathtub, water drowning out the sound of my sobbing, I knew I had a choice: to proceed with fear of certain demise or to fix my eyes on hope.

It was a fleeting five weeks of surgery and treatment that led to the heartbreaking loss of my husband and children's daddy. What followed were years of repeatedly learning to choose gladness and hope over embitterment and despair, an exercise that never truly ends for any of us.

It's easy to cling to our experiences of pain and pooh-pooh gladness bringers, but when we do we forfeit our opportunity for greater joy and happiness. We set ourselves up to merely endure life, when we could actually alter our perceptions and thrive experientially, if not circumstantially.

I understand that staying mindful of how we perceive the world is a constant challenge. One day the world seems bright and sunny, and the next it is riddled with heartache and pain. Nevertheless, if we want to truly be happy, the power is in our own hands.

No one said it would be easy. I need to be reminded of this just as you do, but nevertheless, it's our choice to believe that joy is an inner reality and not an outer one. This is the key to an abundant reality rather than one of scarcity.

Perception Challenge and Exercise

When you hear that same old story rise up in your mind, challenge yourself to reframe your circumstance and engage in the Glad Game, finding something to be glad about in every situation. When you are tempted to preclude possibility by insisting on your version of reality, practice letting go and choosing the possibility of gladness over your pain and disappointment.

Abundance is all in the way you choose to see the world. It begins with letting go of judgment and holding a wide-open space for possibility. This does not mean that I endorse denial of feelings, but directing your feelings in the way you want them to go releases you from internal bondage. Look at reality and make a choice; nurse the bitter side of life, or reframe your experiences into gold. How will you reframe your lens with a gladness infusion?

Uprising! New Belief: It's all in your hands! Wow, that's a daunting thought and an empowering one at the same time. It doesn't mean that you have to will your way through life. It means you're choosing a willing posture to receive the goodness God and the universe have for you. It means you're open to letting your spirit guide you into an upgrade in your perspective and belief system. It means you can always find things to be glad about, knowing that abundance is an inside job! Ask to receive your own personal upgrade, and then expect it!

Repeat out loud: Today I willingly give up the lens I've kept focused on my pain and choose the upgrade of abundance and possibility in my thinking and perspective. This means I choose to reframe difficult circumstances and cultivate a glad outlook. I choose to believe that God has a good plan and I will be better for my experiences. I choose to live from the abundance of gladness and gratitude, rather than fear and lack.

DAY 11: "BUT…" ILLUSION DEBUNKING

How easily we twist stories and situations to fit our sense of being slighted, forgotten, overlooked and devalued. What if none of that was true?

Imagine that the person's sneer from across the room has nothing to do with us. Imagine that our mate's cranky attitude does not reflect upon us. The lies we've believed, which make us ready to pounce on anyone who seems to confirm the notion that we're lacking, are merely a smoke screen that needs to be cleared away.

We know that if we put our hand in a hornet's nest, we might get stung. We can pull the stinger out of our hand, but it's unlikely that we can pull the painful poison out of the hornet. The sting is not about us; we just got in the crosshairs of a person's pain.

Imagine that we're sitting high above our life watching the show and have the advantage of seeing the full picture. Now that sneer from across the room carries with it heartbreak because we can see the torment in the other person's life. Perhaps the person never forgave himself for something he did and is now covered in guilt and shame that he directs onto others. Many people survive by being the victim in their story and blaming the world for their pain.

Once we understand the shame the other person may be carrying, our perceptions and posture begin to shift. This allows us to drop the offense we've carried. It doesn't mean that we need to placate the other person's victim stance, but it means we can be free from being drawn into further drama.

Suddenly the words that pierced to the heart become impotent because we see that outward malice was merely a manifestation of the inward struggle and bitterness they carried for themselves. Recognizing this allows us to make a shift while staying clean in the process.

What if we just didn't take it on? What if we refused to be offended or rejected? What if we refused to replay our story as victim or take part in the us-versus-them game?

Life is made up of relationships, and our relationships are fueled with the energy we bring to them. This means we can foster the powerful, life-giving energy of love or the negativity of fear and resistance. We get to choose.

Perception Challenge and Exercise

Take all of your "But..." and kindly and honestly examine your story that's kept you cycling round and round in an endless loop. Write it out. Get it down on paper. You no longer need to spend your life getting even, requiring retribution and wasting the best of your days on a worn-out-interpretation. You're more than this! We're more than this!

Uprising! New Belief: What if you choose to accept and believe that you're enough? What if you let go of your story and its events? What if you let go of fault and blame and accept every beautiful part of yourself? This is your chance to walk out of the old and into the new. This is your chance to rise up!

Repeat out loud: I am no longer willing to give my life away to a story or illusion of my own making or anyone else's. I am no longer willing to hang on for dear life to an interpretation when I can be free. Today I choose my own freedom.

DAY 12: DO YOURSELF A FAVOR AND LET IT GO

Yesterday we talked about the illusion wrapped up in our well-rehearsed and savored stories. We talked about moving on to freedom. Today we are revisiting this, because our stories tend to have a certain stick-to-itiveness about them that keeps us cycling back around for years. We're coming back to pick up the emotional stragglers that wanted to stay camped out in our pain because it's so darn familiar and honestly comfortable. Often we don't even recognize their presence.

When Mark and I got ready to purchase our home, before much packing or heavy lifting even commenced, I felt so exhausted I couldn't get out of bed. I asked my naturopath about my exhaustion, and she assured me that I was using different muscles and told me not to worry, saying that it was normal.

But I didn't think my tears or exhaustion were normal. I wondered why I wasn't excited or happy about this venture in our lives. After five or more days of feeling terrible, I got curious. "What is going on with you?" I asked.

Taking the time to observe pays off. In this case, I was instantly aware of what I had not seen before: my energy was being drained by my subconscious beliefs. Even though this was a joyful move that we had been anticipating for some time, my subconsciousness had stored painful memories of the many moves I endured as a child, applied them to this scenario and sent me into fight-or-flight mode. Without my awareness, my body had begun to brace itself for another round of transition. It was doing what it had learned to do many years before; it was protecting me from the pain and sadness of more upheaval and loss.

With this new awareness, I immediately began to speak to myself, reassuring the little girl inside who was gearing up for the challenge that this move was a good thing. I wasn't being moved against my will. This was a choice my husband and I had made with intention, and it was thrilling.

Immediately my energy shifted and my extreme fatigue lifted. I began to feel joyful excitement about our new home as my subconscious caught up to speed.

Rehash or Let Go?

As a child, when my parents were navigating the difficulty in their marriage that led to their divorce, I developed asthma, so I became familiar with how much my body picks up on my emotions. It has been said that all unexpressed emotion comes out sideways, and often we fail to recognize the physical connections. The body was created as a magnificent machine; our nervous systems control functions that we pay little attention to, such as breathing, digestion, cell renewal, purifying toxins, balancing hormones, converting stored energy from fat to blood sugar, and on and on. Because our bodies can continue to function through a sort of autopilot, ignored stressors will continue to be triggered long after an actual event if we do not address them.

Our perceptions of experiences create memories that are imprinted in our consciousness, where they can continue to affect our bodies from the inside out long after an actual event. Imagine how those thoughts can continue to affect us.

In *Ageless Body, Timeless Mind*, Deepak Chopra writes about a phenom-
enon seen through psychiatrist Irvin Yalom's experience with an over-
weight patient named Betty. As Betty worked to shed unwanted pounds,
she began to have traumatic dreams of painful incidents in her past. Yalom recognized that she was again experiencing various traumas that oc-
curred in her past at certain weights. Memories from her past were locked
in her unconsciousness, and as her weight hit numeric benchmarks, corresponding traumas that caused her weight gain resurfaced. Her pain was
actually locked within her cells.[3]

Another study Chopra relates noted that laboratory mice, when given repeated mild shocks at random intervals, experienced heightened stress
levels. Each time a mouse was shocked, its body would break down a little,
so that after a few days the mouse would eventually die from stress. The
autopsy reported accelerated signs of aging. The shocks themselves did
not kill the mice, but rather their bodies' reaction to them did.[4]

Chopra tells us, "The very act of paying conscious attention to bodily functions instead of leaving them on automatic pilot will change how you
age."[5] My willingness to investigate my extreme fatigue opened up an entirely new experience through which I let go of an old, subconscious pain.

Several years ago, I experienced healing of a dog allergy when we had the
opportunity to house-sit for a family that owned a dog. I had had a dream
years before, as a precursor to the invitation, in which I was healed of al-
lergies. Because of this dream, I jumped on the house-sitting opportunity
and believed that I was ready to say goodbye to this affliction of stored
pain. The whole time we took care of this dog, I was free from asthma and

3   Deepak Chopra, *Ageless Body, Timeless Mind* (New York: Three Rivers Press, 1993), 289.
4   Chopra, *Ageless Body, Timeless Mind*, 151.
5   Chopra, *Ageless Body, Timeless Mind*, 13.

all dog-related allergy symptoms, and that has stayed true to date. Openness to investigate our inner world can result in outer change.

How We Choose to Process Pain

When we experience pain in the present, we feel it as hurt, but pain in the past can be experienced as anger, while pain or fear of pain in the future creates anxiety. The way we process pain will be reflected in our overall health and aging process because our mind and body are inseparable.

How many thoughts that we're not aware of direct our lives? How much unease is related to unexplored territory within us? It might be time to let go of some old thinking.

Perception Challenge and Exercise

Today you are affirming and determining that you are willing to let it go. This means when a story reasserts itself, you will stop the story in its tracks and say to yourself, "Is this true? Thanks for sharing, but we can move on to the greener pastures of a new perspective."

Take proactive responsibility for how you choose to reframe your story and process your pain. This means you agree to stop rehearsing your pain in your mind or conversation. You're choosing to live life in the present.

Uprising! New Belief: Today is a powerful day of exchange. You get to trade out your pain for freedom. You get to walk out the door of your old story into the world of possibility, and that, my friend, is an uprising if ever there was one. Congratulations! Don't look back except to use your story to empower others.

Repeat out loud: I choose to become aware of the ways my story has affected me on many levels. I choose to address the fears and pain I've buried. I willingly let go of my rights to plead the case that I've been harmed and choose instead the higher path of showing up fully alive to the present moment. I choose to face my fears about letting go of my story and excuses. Today is a good day that is full of new possibilities, and I embrace them.

DAY 13: BREATHE IN PERSONAL HOSPITALITY AND KINDNESS

Last week we talked about the importance of breath to our bodies and to our lives. We considered the message we send our bodies when we hold our breath and withhold the oxygen they so vitally need.

When we trash-talk our self, who's always in earshot of our body, imagine the message we're sending ourselves! This is hurtful and we don't even realize that we're doing it.

Think about what ideas are sinking in when we make passing comments to ourselves like, "You idiot!" or "Why are you so fat and ugly?" What terrible self-abuse we inflict on ourselves!

We would never think of treating someone else we love with such harshness, yet without thought and in numerous ways, we do this to ourselves. We might not even notice these comments because they're ingrained in our thoughts, yet they reveal the resistance felt in our bodies that festers below the surface. Our bodies are craving kindness and self-respect.

Remember how quickly my kindness sank in when I comforted myself around my new home and move? It's as if we're sponges ready and willing to soak up the kindness we're craving from ourselves! Isn't it time we became gracious and generous with personal hospitality and kindness?

Perception Challenge and Exercise

Sit for a moment in silence and contemplate the way personal hospitality would feel in your body. Take a deep breath and breathe into your lungs a generous serving of nurturance, letting it seep into your body, soul and spirit. Imagine it going deep into all the cut-off places that have been resistant to change. Let personal hospitality set up housekeeping throughout your being as if it were a brand spanking new residence, as if it was a new beginning. Sit with this welcome and personal kindness and let the balm of self-love soak into every fiber of your being. This is the way it was always intended to be.

Uprising! New Belief: No one can hold a space of personal hospitality that you do not hold for yourself. You can continue to look out there for the perfect mate, job, environment or friends, but until you become a welcoming environment for yourself, you will not find it elsewhere. This is your chance to rise up, girlfriend. Create a warm place of home and welcome within. Grant yourself personal hospitality.

Repeat out loud: I choose to be a place of personal hospitality for myself. That means I will stop and listen to what I am feeling. I will pay attention when my heart lags behind. I will give myself the same respect that I give to others and even more because I am the caretaker of this vessel. I will speak blessing over myself and love myself tenderly. I cannot do this unless I am willing to sit still, listen and respond to what my spirit is saying. I will breathe in a new kindness and respect for myself today!

DAY 14: UPRISING: DADDY GOODNESS

As humans, we have a tendency toward hyper-independence. It's this vein that frequently blinds us from recognizing how truly connected we are to one another.

In his book *The Divine Dance*, Richard Rohr tells us, "One of the many wonderful things that scientists are discovering as they compare their observations through microscopes with those through telescopes is that the pattern of the neutrons, protons, and atoms is similar to the pattern of planets, stars, and galaxies; both are in orbit, and all is relational to everything else."

Rohr goes on to say, "If a loving Creator started this whole thing, then there has to be a 'DNA connection,' as it were, between the One who creates and what is created...Life flow is the ground of everything, absolutely everything."[6]

Divine Connection

While the Western consciousness has often set God in the distance, detached and indifferent to his creation, there is a global awakening happening in which we are recognizing a connection and similarity between the Divine and humanity in a dance of relationship.

Certainly this connection has always existed, but Rohr explains, "True spirituality should give us access to the bigger field, but it does not seem

---

6   Richard Rohr, *The Divine Dance* (New Kensington, PA: Whitaker House, 2016), 55.

that most of our religions have risen above the tribal level up to now."[7]

This tribal energy Rohr is referring to is a sort of dualistic thinking of "us" and "them" that crept into civilization a long, long time ago and has been reinforced in much of society. This is the cause for the notion of separation. Even our Father and Mother, Adam and Eve, imagined that God had removed himself from them, when in reality their own skewed perspective created the feeling of distance and illusion of separation.

Love?

We still struggle with believing that God is Love, and so we attempt to divide up what God loves and what is delegated to the back lot for punishment. We create elite structures and call them "holy," deceiving ourselves into making God an either-or God when God's relational nature expresses something entirely different.

"God is not first of all a 'being' that loftily decides to love good people and punish bad people; instead, Absolute Love stands revealed as the very name and shape of Being itself," writes Rohr. "Just like the Trinity, we are not a substance, but a relationship."[8]

If we are a relationship and Absolute Love is intertwined within us, it would only make sense that God is operating for us and as us, even imparting and supplying an understanding of the things of God within us.

Rohr tells us that because we've failed to access or understand our own

7   Rohr, *Divine Dance*, 54.
8   Rohr, *Divine Dance*, 78–79.

operating system, our relationship with God has remained immature and superficial, with rote clichés instead of reality. And what's worse is that we've learned to filter our experiences according to what we agree with based on our limited understanding. Certainly that would limit our relationship with God.

Instead of a relationship, we've feasted on secondhand information that's kept us stunted and unable to grow. All mystery becomes static and trapped in dogma and doctrine, rather than being something with life-changing potential. Unless we are willing to question our beliefs and opinions, we will remain unchanged, while the unlimited abundance of God is eclipsed by our shortsightedness. Separation remains the illusion that keeps us blocked and blinded.

Presence Over Logic

Most of us think our way into our beliefs, theology and ideas about God and ourselves. Even in this book, there is much to think about and contemplate. However, the only real way we can actively experience the movement and breath of God in our lives and in our beings is through engagement. We can't think our way there. Contemplation is the means of pulling aside to engage and receive.

Culturally, humans believe in working our way into things, but with God it's the opposite. In truth, we are receptors, not workers.

What child is required to initiate his or her own breath? We simply receive. We're effortlessly hooked up in the womb of life. Oh, the utter ease and freedom of a childlike posture.

All striving and hyper-independence indicate a lack of awareness around being in a relationship and being daddied. It's only when we look in the mirror that we begin to discover who we truly are. We look like our daddy. We look like God and we didn't do anything to make that happen.

Daddying

The wonderful mystery of a divine relationship encompasses a fathering component. Many of us can't see past the absenteeism of our own fathers, and so we struggle to embrace this reality rolled up into divine Love. Yet this connection can't be severed any more than the link of DNA found within us or the umbilical cord that connected us to life within the womb. Connection is who we are, not because we recognize it or belong to the right club, but because of our lineage.

It's only illusion that separates us and makes us forget our True Source. The moment we go off into fear, we close ourselves off further from being able to recognize the undiminishable Love that has always surrounded us, the daddy root that infiltrates us at the core.

Our very reason for existence is to be loved and to be brought into Love. It's the unending circle without beginning or end. It's what we've been swept up into, not as an afterthought, but as an intentional act of love. It's the eternal flow that we can move with or struggle against.

In every crevice of our life, Love's divine DNA is present. It always has been and always will be. Divine Love is the initiator in our lives.

Even if you do have a small inkling of Love's fingerprints upon your coming and going, you might be wondering, how do you recognize this place of relationship, where you flow with what Love is initiating in your life?

Begin in the Present

Many spiritual leaders use words like prayer, contemplation, awe, wonder, observation and curiosity to talk about intersecting with Love's flow. These words, like the nature of the Divine, are intangible; they describe the unfettering and releasing of control that allows us to move into the flow, as in a river.

Cultivating a practice of quieting oneself, sitting still, observing, contemplating and awakening to awe and wonder becomes the place to connect to one's truest self and the Divine. God intertwining within us demonstrates that there's no getting to him without going through us. This is relationship. Often people think of God in terms of things we do, rather than in terms of a connection that comes through relationship. Relationship is the vehicle to engage with God.

Without connecting with the temple in which God dwells—us—we're merely engaging in outer hoopla, tradition and ritual, forfeiting a relationship, the only place where intimacy can occur. To enjoy a relationship with another person, you have to spend time in that person's presence.

Perception Challenge and Exercise

For many, moving past logical thinking to the place of rest and receiving presents a challenge. Ego wants to *do* and make its mark, while receiving is effortless. Thanks to ego, our issue will always be getting out of the way.

You probably have been taken into a bigger field of vision than you've previously seen, yet are struggling with the duality of "us" and "them" thinking that's been your worldview. I challenge you to open your hands and let go of preconceived notions. You can always return to anything you choose. Fear, however, is what will keep you from curiosity, contemplation and an ever-growing perspective.

Take time to journal around these simple questions:

- Did God require your help to get you into the world?

- Did you do anything to receive God's love?

- Does he require you to do what he has not initiated in your life?

Imagine how close the voice is that's already speaking within you. Imagine the sway of the river gently moving you in the right direction, or causing you to pause and sit still. Isn't it time to let go and bend to the direction of the river?

Uprising! New Belief: Today, as you release your fear-driven need for control, open your hands to trust that Love is carrying you into more freedom and peace. Move out of your head into the realm of presence. Willingly stand in the river without needing to drive it.

Be open and rest in this sacred space of intimacy.

Repeat out loud: Today I will get out of my way and open up to wonder and awe over this mystical relationship of Love and Life. I will meditate on God's daddy goodness, because that's who he is, and good daddies love fully. It's here that I can remain in the flow of the river, receiving the bounty of being well cared for. I need only receive instead of forcing the river. I am in relationship found in the very heart of God.

WEEK 3:

Life Is Energy

Day 15: You Attract Your Own Energy

Day 16: Energy This

Day 17: Thankfulness for Now

Day 18: Receive Like a Child

Day 19: Self-Forgiveness Is a Reconnector

Day 20: Breathe In Receptivity

Day 21: Uprising: Bye-Bye Blame

INTRODUCTION TO WEEK 3

Life Is Energy

As we begin Week 3, we are moving further into the never-ending spiral of discovery, where the kaleidoscope opens to new facets and ways of seeing that we might not have considered before. Enter with openness. Each bite-sized portion is just enough to chew on.

If you ever feel overwhelmed with the material, slow down and ask yourself what's going on. Get curious and face your resistance head on. That's what I've done to bring this material to you and continue to do.

When I face a health crisis, I look at what's going on internally. When I face a relationship issue, instead of blaming the other person, I look at what's going on in me and what I can learn. When I face a work crisis, I do the same.

Life is a mirror, but we have to open our eyes to see what's being reflected back at us. We don't live life in a vacuum, so it's important to understand how our consciousness level is affecting not only our lives, but our relationships.

We will continue to explore some of the same topics from various vantage points so that they can truly sink in. We will continue to expand our capacity, and before we know it, we will be experiencing an internal upgrade. Enjoy the journey. Let's dive in and get started!

DAY 15: YOU ATTRACT YOUR OWN ENERGY

Ralph Waldo Emerson reminds us, "Your genuine action will explain itself and will explain your other genuine actions. Your conformity explains nothing."[9] How often are our actions genuine, rather than choices of abdication and conformity?

Oddly, the word *incongruence* sprang up in my spirit and wouldn't let go of me, like a dog on a bone. I had no idea what this Spirit message was referring to until, bit-by-bit, pieces began to be uncovered. I discovered that resistance and incongruence come as a pair.

Resist much? I sure have. One of the ways I came to recognize my own resistance was when a friend of over twenty years gave me one of the greatest gifts I've ever received. She dumped me, but not in a way I initially understood.

In fact, it took two years for it to sink in. My family and I moved away to Los Angeles during one of the worst times of my friend's life, as she navigated through a divorce. When my husband and I moved back, beaten up with our own tails between our legs, there was no warm embrace of welcome from my friend; there was a bouquet of flowery words mingled with distance.

I did what I naturally do: pursued and initiated contact. I tried several times to make amends for any hurt I'd caused or wrongdoing on my part while expressing her importance in my life. Nevertheless, there was no

9   Ralph Waldo Emerson, "Self-Reliance," in *Essays by Ralph Waldo Emerson*, edited by Mary A. Jordan (1841; Boston: Houghton Mifflin, 1907), 94–95.

acknowledgement of hurt or offense, just a business-as-usual posture.

Although the words my beautiful friend uttered sounded appropriate, they lacked sincerity. And that's when I *finally* got it. I stopped listening to the parroted niceties, "Love you and such and such," and recognized that the words weren't accompanied by action to validate or back them up. That's when I began to wake up to the huge incongruence strung through the relationship and my life, like pretty lights high up in the trees, too far out of reach to touch.

The lack of calls, responsiveness or willingness to acknowledge or discuss any hurt or offense I'd caused screamed, "She's just not that into you and just isn't going to allow herself to go there. Let it go!"

Finally I gave myself the merit and respect I deserved by listening to the truth my heart discerned. I looked at reality, halted my magical thinking and stopped being tripped up by the words.

The lack of honest and congruent messages in my relationship with my friend mirrored a similar lack in my relationship with myself. While being good at adulting and engaging in all the right behaviors, I had ignored what I truly felt and instead inserted the appropriate behavior.

Suddenly, through this gift of rejection, I began to hear the whimper in my heart that I'd drowned out with a lifetime of activity and responsibility. The little girl within was screaming to get off the merry-go-round and stop participating in the charade. Deep down within I was saying, "Please don't make me go to that gathering, where I will smile, even though I know that horse is dead, and come home with a deeper laceration in my heart invisible to everyone but me. Please take care of me!"

I recognized that my friend and I were similar in many ways. She was a mirror that allowed me to see myself. I will always be grateful for this gift that came through the back door, as my dutifulness gave way to the sound of my aching heart. It was then that I began to get quiet enough to listen to myself at a much deeper level than I ever had before. I decided to care for myself in an entirely different way instead of "acting" in a manner that was incongruent with what I truly felt. I decided that what I needed was not the love and acceptance of others, but the love and acceptance within myself, right at home, that I had withheld for much too long.

That day I let go of my end of the rope of duty, although my friend had let go long before. When I stopped holding up the rope, it was clear there was nothing left to hold onto anyway.

Until we're willing to look in the mirror, we'll remain caught in incongruence. Recognizing our own double-mindedness helps us release judgment of others, understanding that we all are hindered at times by our own inability to see correctly.

Self-Betrayal

Untold incongruences had been operating in my life, in the saying and doing of the appropriate while betraying myself in the process. This is resistance at its finest, yet few recognize they are dealing with this kind of resistance!

Honestly, I still discover hidden things in my heart of which I've been completely unaware. I've been so well taught and successful at stowing and tucking away feelings that often I fail to recognize what's really there. For most of us, the point is not perfection, but a willingness to acknowledge that caring for everyone else has denied us the deep self-care that we've truly needed for ourselves. Thomas Merton said, "Before we can surrender ourselves we must become ourselves. For no one can give up what he does not possess."[10]

Imagine what it does inside when we feel one way but carry on in an entirely incongruent manner. We might call this hypocritical or dishonest, but most of us don't even recognize what we're doing. It's unintentional. Honestly, it's a common lack of awareness amongst most of the women I know or work with. We all carry varying degrees of inner incongruence.

Wrenching heartbreak can be a great catalyst in helping us discover the ways we've railroaded and prostituted ourselves. If we're willing to listen and respond to ourselves with kindness, instead of cruelly pimping ourselves out to please others, we'll come into true healing and congruence within ourselves.

Not Me?

If you're thinking "This isn't me," remember the time you didn't want to serve on the committee but did it anyway? Remember when you said yes to Aunt Mable because you were afraid to tell her how you really felt? What about the time you did or said (fill in the blank) _____ but didn't want to?

---

10   Thomas Merton, *Thoughts in Solitude* (New York: Farrar, Straus and Giroux, 1999), 29.

As women, in our attempt to be everything everyone else tells us to be, we disconnect from who we are and live in utter personal betrayal. Our need for approval runs so deep that we resist what we think will rob us of it. Freya Madeline Stark said, "There can be no success or happiness if the things we believe in are different from the things we do," and I agree wholeheartedly.

Perception Challenge and Exercise

What if you began to give yourself the approval you've been seeking, knowing that you've already received approval by the mere fact that you exist?

Take some time to become still and inquire of your heart, asking what you might be burying for the sake of acceptance. Listen for the whisper of fear-driven, ego-prompted incongruences. Now spend some time journaling around this.

Imagine the tremendous celebration of letting go of ego's taunt to keep up and look good. Imagine giving yourself permission to acknowledge feelings, thoughts and ideas that you had buried because you thought they would be judged. Imagine the incredible freedom, joy and spaciousness of giving yourself permission to feel how you feel and the kindness to care for yourself.

Write about what it would feel like to walk in this kind of liberty.

Uprising! New Belief: Do you recognize what a gift your recent breakup, job loss or difficult circumstance is giving you? You were gifted the opportunity to connect to yourself in a truer, youer way than ever before.

You have a vast opportunity before you to love yourself in this space of pain, resistance to letting go, incongruence or newly discovered clarity. You can pull up beside yourself with hospitality, love and tenderness, allowing yourself to feel and care for yourself in an entirely new way. Girlfriend, you're on a new trajectory now. You are uprising!

Repeat out loud: I choose to befriend myself and listen for any inner incongruence that causes me to betray myself at the deepest level. Instead of driving myself hard according to my impression of others' opinions and desires, I choose to show kindness to myself. I choose to let myself off the hook for having to be anyone except myself. The illusion of perfection is not something I want to nurse any longer. I am perfectly satisfied with being uniquely and imperfectly me.

DAY 16: ENERGY THIS

Anne Lamott reminds us, "We begin to find and become ourselves when we notice how we are already found, already truly, entirely, wildly, messily, marvelously who we were born to be."[11]

Abundance is an inside job and not a bank account. That being said, I tend to believe that the more we carry an inner abundance, the more it will be reflected outwardly in various ways and possibly even our bank account. I think of this as the overflow.

Having wiped the dirty smears of distrust and disbelief off my lenses, I've been growing in my understanding of what abundance truly means. It was Dr. Caroline Leaf's research about the impact of positive thoughts on the brain that first grabbed my attention years ago.

In her book *Who Switched Off My Brain?* she describes the brain on happy thoughts looking like a flourishing green tree, while conversely the brain on negative thoughts looks like a scorched, mangled thorn bush.[12] Imagine the eroding effect of feeding our brains with horrible stories of deceit, deficit, negativity and pain.

---

11   Anne Lamott, "Becoming the Person You Were Meant to Be: Where to Start
," *O, The Oprah Magazine*, November 2009.

12   Caroline Leaf, *Who Switched Off My Brain?* (Nashville, TN: Thomas Nelson, 2009), 114.

Energy 101

During my life coach training, I was introduced to a greater look at the way energy shows up in our lives. The idea of energy is not merely a woo-woo notion celebrated by hippies. We know scientifically that the world is made up of energy, you and me included.

I've retold a few stories about the way negative energy has affected my life and body. This low-level energy is referred to as catabolic energy. Positive energy is called anabolic energy. Just as Dr. Leaf confirmed through brain scans, anabolic energy is restorative and constructive, while catabolic energy erodes and destroys. That's a gold mine of information right there as we glean the powerful effects our thoughts have on our lives.

The founder of the Institute for Professional Excellence in Coaching, Bruce D Schneider, created a scientifically backed assessment to measure one's consciousness or energy levels called the Energy Leadership Index.

Energy and consciousness levels are not fixed, but expand and change according to the way we direct our thoughts and beliefs. The Energy Leadership Index assessment is a remarkable tool to make us aware of the energy in our lives and how we use it.

I'm going to give you a brief introduction to the insights offered by Schneider, a mentor I have worked with personally. What follows is my interpretation of his work. If you'd like to look into it further, I recommend Schneider's book, *Energy Leadership*.[13]

13   Bruce D Schneider, *Energy Leadership* (Hoboken, NJ: Wiley, 2008).

You've Got Energy

The Energetic Self Perception Chart details the seven measurable levels of energy, revealing core thoughts and emotions that result in actions. Interestingly, the results of society at large fall predominately in the two lowest levels of catabolic energy. This is not hard to believe after witnessing the current political and social climate in the U.S. and the world. Sadly, insults, disrespect, lying, blame casting, judgment and accusation are the norm these days.

What I've just described are the attributes of Level 2 energy, but let's start with Level 1.

Level 1: Victim

The core thought at Level 1 is victim thinking and the core emotion is apathy, which results in lethargy, fear, ego, faithlessness, unconsciousness and neediness. At this level, we see despair, despondency and hopelessness and feel powerless to change. Whew, I've been in this level in my life more often that I care to recall, and as research suggests, so have you!

Level 2: Conflict

Level 2 comprises the core thought of conflict, which elicits the emotion of anger and moves into defiance, blame and conflict. If you took the assessment today, you would most likely be surprised to find yourself with scores that include these lowest energy levels. But you're not alone.

The reason this energy is so toxic is not only because it's an outward affront, often polluting the atmosphere of those around us, but also be-cause of the negative stress hormones it releases into our own bodies. This energy can also show up through repressed and passive-aggressive anger. That's why we talked about inner incongruence and the importance of self-care and personal alignment yesterday. This is something we all struggle with and need to examine daily.

Although Level 2 energy is just as negative as Level 1, it's actually moving one step closer to positive anabolic energy. Although it often creates a neg-ative environment, it creates momentum for movement, which ultimately can produce positive results. Think of a stern boss, parent or even laws put forth to provide consequences and direction for change. Sometimes we need a kick in the rear, but we don't want to consistently live from this life-draining energy. Think: burnout!

Often we see Level 2 energy functioning in politics, corporations and even families. This energy keeps us vying for control, creating the need to blame and scapegoat others instead of seeking a win-win in life. This is not an empowering energy.

The Circle of Life

Schneider's Energetic Self Perception Chart is circular. Think of Level 1 as being the center of the circle. Each level thereafter cycles outward, pro-gressing ultimately toward more expansive, unlimited and unending Love.

With that in mind, the first step to shift out of negative energy and into positive anabolic energy is to take responsibility. And that brings us to Level 3.

Level 3: Responsibility

Level 3 energy carries the core thought of responsibility, which moves into the core feeling and emotion of forgiveness and leads to actions such as cooperation, outer faith and the beginning of awareness. Taking responsibility for one's thoughts, attitudes and actions is a powerful step toward change and growth.

Taking Ownership

I am proud to be a coach and proud of the energy around coaching that helps people shift into personal responsibility, ownership and ultimately higher levels of consciousness. Responding to life with anabolic energy enables us to climb out of difficulty and rise when we've fallen.

Each energy level moves us up into a higher consciousness, attitude and perspective that shifts our core thoughts, emotions and outcomes in life. This can be felt inwardly and seen outwardly, both individually and in society as a whole. Society exemplifies where we individually resonate, and that is why change always begins with self.

Level 4: Compassion

In Level 4 we begin to see compassion as a core thought and concern as the core emotion, and the result is service to others. This opens us to empathy and the beginning of standing in another's shoes. However, at Level 4, people sometimes get stuck and camp out fixing or valuing empathy above all else. While compassion can give us a higher shift in perspective and energy, we need to watch out for a hypersensitivity so as not to be derailed back into Level 1.

Level 5: Peace

Level 5 moves us to the core thought of reconciliation, the core emotion of peace and the result of acceptance. Imagine how important this is in our lives. It's easy to identify when we recognize and align to this energy because we let go of struggle. Ingenuity and new ideas begin to emerge from this level. Vision is birthed and we perceive life from a win-win perspective all around.

Level 6: Joy

Level 6's core thought is synthesis, the core emotion joy, and the result is wisdom. Levels 6 and 7 move from outer faith to inner faith, and we witness the absence of ego and a delving into consciousness opposed to unconsciousness. I believe at this level we experience the powerful reality of unhindered freedom.

Level 7: Absolute Passion

The ultimate level, Level 7, is like nirvana. Although neither this nor any other level is fixed or stationary, Level 7 could be described as the ebb and flow of Spirit. The core thought at Level 7 is non-judgment and the core emotion is absolute passion, with the result being creation. For those in this place, everything flows from ultimate Love.

You can see how the higher energy levels not only affect relationships and our ability to navigate through them, but also our worldviews, our own wellbeing and our ability to innovate in every possible manner. The two lowest levels of energy merely destroy and tear down others and ourselves.

It's easy to recognize that nearly every spiritual leader revered in the world did or does function from higher energy levels: Jesus, Buddha, Gandhi, Martin Luther King Jr., Mother Teresa, Nelson Mandela, Desmond Tutu—and the list goes on.

Society often defines success through outer gain, but greater love, joy, happiness and peace are the ultimate definitions of success. You can see the importance of abundance and scarcity in our thinking and worldview. Isn't it empowering to know that we can recognize our energy and learn to shift it?

Don't be overwhelmed by the discovery of negative energy in your life because, as you know by now, we all have learned to cope and persevere through various means, which have often supported low energy. However, we can now celebrate greater awareness and the freedom to shift our energy!

As you've just learned, taking responsibility is the first step into positive energy and each level thereafter opens up the space of greater possibility, spiritual connection and the flow of divine relationship. Energy isn't static, but an ever-moving current that can continue to expand in our lives in greater degrees.

Perception Challenge and Exercise

Today, take some time to investigate where you see toxic catabolic energy showing up in your thoughts, beliefs and actions. Is your health revealing what might not be apparent otherwise? My health often signals to me what's going on beneath the surface that I may not be aware of. Our energy presents a great invitation for inquiry.

Journal about your discoveries and the shifts you'd like to see in your energy and perspective. This may be a big eye-opener; you may never view the world through the same lens again, but instead grow in increasing forgiveness, compassion, peace, joy, synthesis, wisdom and love.

Uprising! New Belief: Now you can see why the energy we reflect comes back to us. When we stay in the flow of Spirit, we will operate from higher energy and attract the same energy back. While we are in fear, resistance and scarcity will continue to show up all around us. What we see from the energy of love will be very different from the negativity of conflict and victim energy.

Are you inspired to look in the mirror yet? Let it reflect back to you your reality. Instead of struggling with what you see, why not get in the river and let the water direct you into a vaster, more abundant perspective and reality?

Repeat out loud: Today, I see that I truly am the guardian of my own energy, and with Spirit as my guide, I can release the toxic negative thoughts, emotions and energy that manifest in my life. There is no hoop to jump through, merely recognition, responsibility and receptivity. I am an open vessel and therefore can move from one energy to the next effortlessly, as I'm open to the flow.

DAY 17: THANKFULNESS FOR NOW

One morning I woke up and noticed the absence of joy. I began to take a deeper look and realized that there was a sort of low-grade anxiety swirling beneath the surface. Granted, there was a lot going on. We were feverishly compiling massive amounts of paperwork for the purchase of our home and repeatedly resending it in corrected formats after the initial submissions didn't meet the test! We were redesigning our future kitchen and bathrooms and researching appliances, cabinets and flooring—not to mention that I was planning my upcoming Untamed Creative Women's Retreat.

Suddenly I said to myself, "I don't want to feel this way. I want to feel giddy! We are about to close on our new home and hello, that is thrilling!" I began thanking God for all the goodness in my life, and in an instant I began to feel giddiness stir up within my being. Butterflies began to swirl in my stomach and a smile emerged across my face. I became giddy to the point of silliness. I called my hubby and dropped a silliness bomb on him too! Talk about shifting energy!

This may seem overly simplistic to the person struggling with illness, disaster, disappointment, betrayal or despair. And I by no means intend to make light of anyone's pain. I have lived through significant heartbreak, and the way I rose out of it time and time again was making a choice about the way I wanted to perceive and live my life.

Later this same day, I reflected back on my initial swirl of anxiety and connected it to, yep, resistance and fear. In the midst of all the wonderful busyness of life, I was nervous about filling my upcoming retreat. Suddenly I began to recognize my resistance and fear related to the work that I do and love tremendously.

Suddenly the lights began to come on. I knew that the giddiness shift I had experienced earlier in the day was applicable in any circumstance, and so I began to let it rise up a little higher within my being.

Here's what I identified: fear and resistance are universal. We can be sure we are in fear or resistance when we aren't feeling well; there's an absence of joy and our heart is troubled.

This is when we need to kindly and honestly observe what's going on and determine the ways in which resistance is showing up and what we're resistant to. When low energy surfaces, there's usually something we want, believe we are lacking or think we can't have, and so we focus on the gaping lack, rather than trusting and believing in an ample source of Love and supply.

In my case, I want to feel fully valued, embraced, celebrated and sought after in my work supporting women, but until I am able to fully celebrate, embrace and value this part of myself (being a boss lady), I'll remain in a place of fear, scarcity, lack and resistance. My distrust and disbelief keeps me in a place of low energy and scarcity.

If I believe that I need "clients" to be successful, I immediately give my power away. The truth is that I don't need anything outside of myself to be successful. Nothing outside of myself defines me or my success or is a measure of my worth. Our worth is already settled, and the more we awaken to this reality that we always have been and always will be fully loved and accepted, the more we get an immediate upgrade in our perception and the more our energy shifts.

Focusing on something that we believe to be out of reach keeps us in fear and a victim state, rather than believing that we are enough right now. When we shift our focus from "not enough" to gratitude for what we have right now, even seemingly mere crumbs, our energy shifts. Gratitude is the ultimate shifter.

When we see an area of our life where scarcity, resistance and fear are showing up, we need to check in and observe. Thoughts and feelings of fear and lack simply reveal an illusion, a belief that we're separated from Love and the ultimate Love Source, which creates fear and anxiety. The truth is, there is nothing that can separate us from Love except our minds.

When we project our need onto something or someone else, we are implying that that thing or person is our source. Nothing could be further from the truth.

When we choose to let go of the illusion and feelings of separation that are tied up with our story, we can begin to move into the truth and reality of being completely loved and supplied with everything we need.

And here is the crux of it: We need to live from a reality bigger than the hand in front of our face. We need to live from an expanding, ongoing, unending vantage point, taking today in stride, because the story isn't finished. That's faith!.

Perception Challenge and Exercise

Today, you get to challenge your areas of ingratitude and pull back from your close-up interpretation of events and circumstances that you're only seeing in part. You get to choose to be thankful and believe that you're fully cared for, loved and supplied in all things. When doubt, negativity or fear pops up, you get to choose to meet it head-on with a thankful heart that sees past the fleeting moment into the expanse of eternity.

You might be thinking, "How do I do that?" You begin by sitting still, closing your eyes and imagining yourself standing in the river, if you like. Everything is flowing toward you and moving out through you. You are surrounded and moving with the flow. There is no lack as you are touched by life on every side. There is no way to escape this teeming life except to withdraw from it. Nevertheless, it will not go away if you do. You will merely perceive that it has gone.

In this way, move out beyond your momentary difficulty and focus on the expansiveness of Love. Over time you will begin to realign yourself with gratitude by focusing your attention on unending Love. Begin practicing today.

Uprising! New Belief: Your attitude is fueled by your thoughts, perception and beliefs, all of which can be upgraded at any time. You can move into as much abundance as you can handle when you allow for an upgrade in energy and thinking. It all starts with a thankful heart that can identify the ample abundance that exists in your life right now, the abundance of Love surrounding you that you've been blinded to.

Wade out into the river and get submerged in this wealth of Love engulfing you. Dive in, get wet and see the vastness all around. Enter into your upgrade!

Repeat out loud: I will not base my worth, identity or state in life on external factors. I am grateful that I woke up today to breathe in another day of life, to see the flowers in bloom, hear the birds sing and to believe in the goodness of God that made me and upholds me. I am grateful for all I have and I will focus my attention on the goodness of Love instead of areas of perceived lack.

DAY 18: RECEIVE LIKE A CHILD

My ego worked me into becoming a doer. My personality type is naturally task-oriented, and I feel accomplished when I can mark things off my list. For a long time, this mode of operation seemed acceptable. It was acceptable and looked darn good, until I recognized my repeated adrenal fatigue and burnout.

I've coached clients that have told me they feel powerful when they receive accolades and praise for their accomplishments, even though they're living with constant stress and anxiety. Hmm... is this healthy?

Our ego isn't creative. It's linear and can only focus on what gives the illusion of control. Real inspiration and creativity are the result of letting go of control and receiving. Remember the higher energy levels that usher in greater innovation, acceptance, synthesis and peace?

It's taken me a long time to differentiate between my intent to strive, perform, get 'er done and execute, on the other hand, and a very different posture of openness and willingness to receive organically and divinely from a higher level of consciousness.

Sometimes the ability to execute is important and a positive step toward moving forward. However, because the universe never ceases to create, everything in life opens up to us when we're able to receive and believe that we're being supported supernaturally. Creativity works through openness rather than control.

The posture of receiving is childlike. Children are masters at receiving without questioning the supply. Young children dance and play their way into creating all day long. They sing about their work, "We are getting in the car to run errands," and with open hands are led on continuous adventures.

When we are open to receiving, it shifts the way we face our day. Moving about like we're killing snakes creates toxic energy. At any time, we can position ourselves like a child to joyfully receive all that the universe wants to give us.

Of course, we first have to give up suspicion and the notion that everything has to be hard. We have to expect good and foster kind, internal self-talk like the sing-song goodness that children do. "I am cared for today. I can walk out my door believing that I will receive everything I need because I am open to receive and I am fully loved and supplied."

Hang out with young children and you will be inspired by their ability to observe and quickly move into creative thinking, creating games on the spot, or plays, songs or artwork. You name it. Kids are masterful at observing, receiving inspiration and creating.

Our eavesdropping cells are effortlessly being imprinted upon by our thoughts, be they joy, happiness, angst or resistance. Yet most of the time, we're oblivious to the fact that we've let something imprint upon us. We fail to be in the state of observation or face our circumstances with wonder and awe.

Just a few seconds of recognition around our energy and thoughts can shift us out of the familiar, well-worn groove of autopilot we've adopted and into an entirely new paradigm. Even if it takes more than one redirection to shift entirely, we could momentarily experience a burst of joy and positivity.

Why do we hold on so tightly to negativity and struggle instead of making the shift? It's because it takes the innocence of childlike faith to do so. It requires exercising trust and believing that there is goodness in the world that is directed toward us, despite what our familiar tapes are rehearsing.

We often pride ourselves on weighing the scales and making realistic assessments. But how has that worked for us? We're guarded, unhappy and immoveable.

However, if we open ourselves up to *receive* the abundance available to us, we just might find miraculous things are being drawn to and supplied for us. Even faith can be supplied to us as we open ourselves up to receive it. It all starts with a willingness to observe and open up to inspiration that leads us into a divine upgrade.

It takes that childlike posture of wide-openness to begin to shift our limited beliefs, perspectives and, ultimately, circumstances. The good news is that we can choose the intoxicating posture of glee and unquestioning faith that makes children a delight to be around.

Perception Challenge and Exercise

Today you're going to start getting comfortable with receiving. You're going to strengthen your receptivity muscles, and instead of placing value on slaving away in our adult world, you have the option of believing that as you work, you're being fully and divinely supported.

This means you're willing to let go of equating high productivity with worth. Rather, you value being a creative, intuitive being that *receives* divine support and guidance. More than that, you carry the divine nature, so you're highly intuitive and innovative. You need not pull life by the rope with your bare hands if you're willing to stand in the river, experience it and let it flow to and through you organically.

Uprising! New Belief: There is either abundance or lack. God is either generous or stingy, but not two-faced as many have accused. Choosing to believe and trust in a kind and generous God alters the way you view the world. Viewing the world from abundance attracts much greater possibility and creative inspiration than believing in and focusing on a withholding and stingy Creator.

Continuing to embrace a childlike nature of trust and the ability to receive is a powerful shift that will take you places that being a workaholic with burnout never could.

Be kind and patient with yourself in the process. It will eventually take you into believing and receiving what is truly your birthright. Welcome to an upgrade in beliefs and ultimately a great uprising!

Repeat out loud: I am willing to change my mind about the value of striving. I am open to becoming comfortable with receiving in my life. I believe I am fully supported and loved by God, and so I will align myself to this grand kindness and generosity. I will observe, trust and begin to shift out of negativity and into joy, speaking to myself in the same kind manner and with the openness of a child. I will speak blessings over myself. I am fully blessed and able to receive ample goodness in my life, because God is good and I am fully loved.

DAY 19: SELF–FORGIVENESS IS A RECONNECTOR

Most of the folks that need deep, personal self-forgiveness fail to recognize it. Sometimes the story we've accused ourselves of, such as "being the problem that made such and such run away," or the self-written verdicts we've given ourselves of "terrible parent," "inept failure," or many other labels that we've deemed unforgivable, play on repeat.

And so this hot spot, this delicate little trigger, gets tripped time and time again when it's reinforced from the outside in. It takes some time and deep recognition to bring awareness to the inside where the trigger hides.

It doesn't really matter what the story is because each of our triggers is painful. Fear is intimidating, and so we try to avoid it at all costs, staying stuck in resistance. Every time our button gets triggered, fear starts to holler and we start our dance to manage it. All the "being misunderstood" songs and dances play loudly, keeping us a prisoner, powerless in the face of our triggers.

Instead of staying with the "misunderstood and unheard" storyline, self-forgiveness begins when we give ourselves the understanding and attentive listening that we crave from others. It's turning around and saying, "I hear you, baby girl!"

Our story of feeling abandoned and not belonging changes in an instant when we give ourselves the deep sense of welcome and acceptance we crave. This is self-forgiveness. This is letting go of blaming ourselves and reflecting that blame outwardly onto others. This is a wholehearted, wiping-the-slate-clean embrace of acceptance that helps us let go and forgive ourselves.

This is a lifelong practice, which must be done anew every day. And it all starts as we're willing to become still and observe our emotions and re-actions. When we show up with curiosity, wonder and awe, we will begin to discover untold secrets and new things about ourselves. We'll hear our heart as we stop to listen to Spirit's tender conversations, revealing us to ourselves.

Perception Challenge and Exercise

Today you get to focus on granting yourself the self-forgiveness that you've wanted someone else to give you, but only you can give yourself. Today you can move into a big, wide-open space of release and freedom.

Today, take some time to practice quieting yourself and sitting still in a new spaciousness you will hold for yourself. It is a space of non-judgment and total embrace. It's a place of pardon and kindness that rallies behind you. This is what you've outwardly been seeking and can now find within yourself. Practice a big, tender and welcoming yes to yourself.

Uprising! New Belief: What big strides you've made as you've willingly moved off the well-entrenched belief that's held you for so long. You're willing to give up the belief that you are misunderstood. Now you're free to move back into the true identity you've always carried but forgot when you settled for what was far beneath you. Welcome home, baby girl!

Repeat out loud: I let myself off the hook for whatever I've believed about myself and accused myself of. Today I am free from this merry-go-round and I can jump off it and join the party. Today the illusion of "misunderstood, unheard and unseen" stops because I am showing up and giving myself the warm reception I deserve and have needed from myself. This choice deserves a hallelujah party and so I'll dance in my kitchen!

DAY 20: BREATHE IN RECEPTIVITY

For those of us who have given birth, we understand how that transition makes everything feel wonky and off-kilter. Sometimes the fight and determination increases, only to disappear at a moment's notice. It can take quite a while to get our legs back. But that's what takes place when we're in the process of growing, being stretched and discovering something newer than we've previously experienced. That's the nature of birthing.

It took Mark and me some time (a long time of transition) to figure out what we wanted and where we wanted it after landing back in Charlotte after three years in California. It took six years of wonkiness, plus the new normal of being empty nesters, to boot. Those years felt like a steep mountain of isolation with little reprieve until we suddenly landed smack-dab in the middle of my heart's desire.

During our transition and shifts, there was a feeling of being unseen and unheard in many various forms, as if we were tucked away in a womb, struggling to navigate and see clearly. Relate?

It felt like we were stuck in transition and unable to deliver what we'd been carrying. Initially the temptation rose to find someone to blame for our pain instead of letting the pain grow us. Over time the temptation dwindled as we moved into acceptance, finding joy in the little things and letting go of expectation.

We Are Mirrors

As we've talked about previously, we are our own mirror for what exists in our lives, and that is one of the greatest lessons we can learn from our pain. It's challenging and hard to swallow sometimes, but what we are putting out we're getting back. Learning to stop projecting our pain onto others helps us start healing. The problem is not *them*, it's a reflection of our own lives.

As I started wrestling with my own negativity, choosing to believe in more than I could see in the current situation, and giving thanks for solutions and manifestations long before they arrived, my reality began shifting in one area after another. And as it did, one of my longtime heart's desires to be part of a loving community immediately began to materialize.

And so we bought a house with no idea that we'd find ourselves plopped in the middle of a warm and incredibly social, eclectic neighborhood. Folks of all ages and walks of life welcomed us and ushered us into a well-established party-throwing culture, sort of the neighborhood of my dreams!

When we attended our first party, we met young and old, black and white, gay and straight folks loving each other and getting together regularly. I couldn't believe that this was our new neighborhood! This was effortless.

I went home that night with a sense of party-satisfied amazement and a smile across my face that wouldn't quit. Unbeknownst to us, the universe had been at work right under our noses in rolling out a longtime dream.

Over the years I have certainly tried to initiate and create connection, because I'm an activator. I like action! Some seasons there were pockets of warm friendship and fellowship, while other times it felt forced, stiff and painfully uncomfortable.

There is nothing quite like gratefully experiencing a little slice of heaven that comes in an unexpected way, a gift rather than the result of work. I know that some women have had painful difficulty conceiving, but even with medical assistance we have little to do with creating a life inside us (aside from the fun part). Imagine facing all aspects of life with the same ease of reception, knowing that the best things in life are gifted effortlessly.

Why Does It Take So Long?

Wouldn't it be nice if we could bypass difficult seasons of transition and the pain of birthing? But if we did, we might forfeit some of the most wonderful gifts and surprises wrapped up amidst them.

If we're patient and able to mine for the gold, difficult seasons carry with them a hidden treasure. I believe we can process through difficulty as quickly as we're able to move past our resistance and fear.

When we focus on the goodness towards us, we won't spend our energy cycling around negativity, misguidedly guarding and protecting ourselves. We won't turn to off-loading our unmet expectations onto others, blaming or hiding out, because we will remain in a receptive posture. Shifting our insecurity into positive energy can feel challenging. Nevertheless, we can choose to look for the positive or cling to the negative as much as we want

You might be asking, "Kimber, why the redundancy on our thought life, energy and receptivity?" Because this stuff pops up daily, if not minute to minute! We need to actively tune in to our inner atmosphere in order to shift it and to acknowledge the care we need. With that in mind, the ultimate self-care is the ability to receive. This means we receive help from others, which is a challenge in itself for highly independent folks. And most importantly, we receive from Source and our own being. How open are you to receive?

Perception Challenge and Exercise

What are the areas in which you struggle to receive? The answer will always be where you are stuck in resistance and fear. This means when ego pops up to run the show, you're struggling to receive. This means when a victim or blaming posture makes an entrance, you're struggling to receive.

Spend time journaling around areas where you're due for some super-natural support. Imagine what it would be like to get out of your way, receive divine assistance and flow with the river.

Uprising! New Belief: When I was a widow with four young children, men ran for the hills at the thought of engaging with me! I credit the gift of my husband as supernatural. When we are able to receive, there's no telling what we might receive. How open are you to receiving what you can't create on your own?

Repeat out loud: I stand open and ready to receive. Instead of forcing my way through various transitions in life, I will bend to the movement of the river. I will receive its precious gifts in winter, springtime, summer and fall. I will be open to receiving help from heavenly places. I will believe in the miracles that are scripted from a totally different playbook than I can even imagine!

DAY 21: UPRISING: BYE–BYE BLAME

I'll admit it: I was a blamer. We all have been. When I see images of Jan Brady, "Life's just not fair!" I cringe because at times I've been stuck in the middle child cliché.

Even though blame keeps us powerless, it becomes a safe and comfortable way of life for many folks because it gives us an excuse to avoid taking responsibility for ourselves. Redirecting our pain onto someone else bolsters the illusion that we're powerful, but in truth this low-level reaction to pain is the opposite of powerful. Blame reveals that we're in resistance.

Blame and ego do their best work through relationships. Rarely do we bump up against a struggle that doesn't involve another human being. Blame is ego's resistance strategy and a relational nightmare.

It's said that we can choose to be happy or to be right. How many of us choose the self-righteous route of ego and the need to be right? How often do we place ourselves in the middle of an argument because ego craves the win?

Ego loves to protect and project itself through judgment, comparison and the fundamentals of dualistic thinking: "us" and "them." Ego makes "them" the scapegoat and "us" the righteous victim, or whatever spin we've chosen.

I've mentioned the political divide in the U.S. that's swept across the landscape, bringing with it insult slinging and blame projecting from both sides of the aisle via social media. Ego refuses to hold the space for differences and insists on the angry, catabolic posture of standing against.

When we come from ego, we're operating on a low catabolic energy level where we fail to honor and value other human beings. When we operate from a place of treating others with dignity and respect, as we would like to be treated, we hold the space for differences without attacking others.

This means recognizing that we've come from the same Source. We all came into the world as helpless infants in the womb of creation, the result of a power greater than ourselves. Without acknowledging a divine Source, we will not be able to hold a nonjudgmental, non-elitist posture. It's Spirit that points out ego's judgment, arrogance and bitterness.

Separation

It is the illusion of separation from others and divine Love that keeps us seeking completeness outside ourselves. Ego works to measure feelings of superiority (or lack thereof, depending on the circumstance) while elevating or debunking another and doling out portions of love. Sometimes ego casts us to bottom billing and we don't even make our own list! That's when we assert ourselves through a defend-and-attack posture.

When we place our happiness and value in the hands of something that can shift at any moment, we're creating instability that will always falter. With the illusion that another person or thing outside ourselves can compensate for our sense of lack, we give others our power, rather than grasping the reality that we were never separated from Love in the first place.

Ultimately this framework is built upon self-preservation, which is ego's MO. When we feel vulnerable or threatened, we have uniquely designed (not so unique) methods to defend and protect ourselves. As long as we stay in a defensive posture of blame and attack and remain unaware of our fear, we're stuck in reoccurring patterns, stories from the past and barriers of defense. But all that we're protecting is our ego!

Needless to say, this keeps us in a catabolic state, negatively rehearsing offenses and cycling unresolved issues into new relationships. I'd say that none of us are exempt from recycling round and round some form of unresolved issues that have become the lens through which we see the world.

Upholding Victim

Being a victim can be so darn comfortable that it becomes unrecognizable. That's why it's a well-played card. To support being the victim, we must continue to doubt others and place blame. I don't know about you, but I would much rather choose happiness over this terrible fear-and ego-driven cycle of being right and rehashing my woes. There is nothing more physically draining than uninvestigated stories riddled with fallacy and unforgiveness.

This is why I am determined to address the many illusions I hold that cause me to trip up. When life hands me these opportunities, as if on the silver platter of circumstance, if I'm wise I'll recognize them, grow and change. That's one of Spirit's grand methods of assistance.

Staying in the victim stance is a relational landmine that keeps us stuck in resentment. Failure to forgive sets us up to fail relationally. Who can navigate this kind of sensitive ground with someone who wakes up believing that the world is against them and that they aren't enough?

Moving Out of Blame

How do we move out of blaming patterns when we've spent so many years believing "they" and "all that's been done to me" are the problem? The only way out is a willingness to let go of the pain and the story, while adamantly choosing to forgive.

Sometimes we need a period of detox from situations and relationships that trigger us in negative ways. By stepping back, we can disarm the trigger. I've often told clients if someone's sending a message that they're "just not that into you," listen.

Leaning into what makes us feel alive, rather than relationships and situations that withhold or drain the life from us, will help us stay out of blame, victimhood and cycles that rob us of our dignity and wellbeing. The good news is that we get to choose to let go rather than live in martyrdom.

Once we grow our ability to nurture our self, we won't be triggered so frequently. Once we begin to access the kindness and acceptance that have always been there for us, we will find them overflowing within, regardless of others' outward attitudes toward us. Then the stream of Love will flow unhindered to us and from us. That's the goal, right?

Relational Snags

When we hit upon a relational snag, we easily fall for the lie that God or another is somehow withholding life, opportunity or love from us. We look outwardly for validation, feeling unseen or unvalued. But Love never changes its unending flow—we merely fail to recognize it.

When we stop judging others or ourselves and recognize that not one is greater or lesser than another, we open the way to the truth of being fully loved. God's Love didn't move. Ultimately, all fear and resistance trails back to a profound lack of belief in being fully sourced in the Love of God. Letting go of blame requires a willingness to believe that there is no separation from Love. This is the ultimate energy shift.

Perception Challenge and Exercise

Today I challenge you to look at the relationships that trip you up. Instead of placing blame on the other parties, practice letting go of the victim stance and seeing the other as fully sourced and covered in unconditional Love. Practice acknowledging the paradox of your very humanness that contains divine deposits.

When you find yourself in the terrible throes of judgment, you can easily discern that it's not what you want to feel. Who would want to feel that negative, draining, toxic energy that ultimately leaves you feeling marooned and alone?

Observe how you might be exhibiting the same trait or behavior you've judged in another. How might the other person be a mirror of yourself? Practice seeing yourself as one with others, where there is no separation from the unending River of Love.

Revisit the exercise of letting go of ego every time you find yourself in judgment. Practice observing. Let go of self-judgment and put yourself back into the ease and receptivity of the River. Remind yourself that happiness is better than being right, and that ultimately happiness does not exist without connection to the ultimate Love flow.

Uprising! New Belief: As you continue to reinforce the belief that there is no separation from Love, you are moving away from the need to blame, judge, measure and deflect your own responsibility. The more fully you sink down into being fully loved, the fuller your capacity will be to live from love, rather than the negative effects of blame and a victim mentality. You're in charge of the love you feel; simply embrace it instead of giving your power to some outside source. Take hold of your uprising!

Repeat out loud: I would rather be happy than right, so I choose to see others as fully covered in love, no greater or lesser than myself. I release being a victim and choose to take responsibility to forgive. I invite the Spirit to lead me on the journey of seeing everything as a whole, rather than dualistically.

WEEK 4:

Welcoming the Space Between

INTRODUCTION TO WEEK 4

Welcoming the Space Between

As we learned last week, our consciousness level pertains to the way we see the world. And from there it affects everything in our lives. On a larger scale, each of our consciousness levels contributes to the consciousness level of humankind.

When we stand pointing our finger outwardly, I've heard it said that the other three fingers are pointing back at us. As we judge and point out another's error, the plank in our own eye blinds us from the error in ourselves.

Part of seeing correctly is removing our own plank, which often comes about through life's process of humbling and emptying us of our superfluous clutter, arrogance and ignorance. In fact, it's entirely necessary to be emptied of ego's falsehood, blindness and insincerity before we can truly be filled. Ultimately, through emptying we arrive at our fullest capacity.

There are many space holders in our lives that take up room and block a greater awareness of the things that truly matter. We pay homage to false gods without even realizing it. This week we'll explore the space holders that occupy our time and the thoughts that are standing in our way.

DAY 22: YOUR PATH HAS ALWAYS BEEN HERE

Recently I watched an adorable three-year-old and was reminded of our similarities. With a three-year-old, you never have to wonder what they're thinking. This one's warm snuggle to my leg and endearing "I like your minty smelling perfume" abruptly turned sour a moment later with a shriek of "That smells horrible."

I was ingratiated with a tender hug and then snubbed as passionately. If I'm honest, that's often how I feel and oftentimes how I behave. For all my mature and upright posture, sometimes I forget that I can be as fickle as a three-year-old.

It's this tendency (you have it too) that keeps us spinning and reaching for things that, in the end, fail to satisfy. We move forward with mother-may-I speed, only to move five steps backwards into indecisiveness and dissatisfaction.

Recently at an art gathering, several folks asked if I was participating in further studio classes this year. I mentioned that instead of moving forward with my regular routine, I was taking a hiatus to discern how I landed at this juncture. I wanted to see what had juice in it and was being divinely initiated in my life.

When I got home, I thought about how much the passing comment I had shared four or five times seemed to resonate with people and offered them permission to choose the same option. Granted, this was a group of artists with a tendency to be spiritually intuitive, but the lesson rings true. We don't always listen for the right timing, but often move ahead without wisdom or insight, only to feel our way impeded. Finding our right path takes intention.

I think I might want that opportunity, but do I really? Today, that guy will make me happy, but I'm not sure about tomorrow. Yes, I'll be your friend until it inconveniences me or the minty smell of your essential oil becomes an irritant. Things like your humanness bother me and on and on! Fickle? Yes, I am!

Often We Find Our Path by Discovering What Isn't Our Path

I raise this topic of fickleness not to shame us, but to help us appreciate the process. At first sniff we like the perfume, but do we really? Ultimately we determine that we don't! Bravo! We're defining and evaluating what matters to us.

I wish I could tell you all of the things I thought I wanted, only to discover they did not provide happiness or satisfaction and were only passing fancies.

There was one particular time in my early twenties when I was most profoundly mistaken. I met a Harvard grad who glamorized her choice to be a stripper as if it came through enlightenment. I thought, "Hey, I'm young, cute and like to dance and make money in the process. This is a no-brainer!"

I was hired at one glance, given a stage name and put on the schedule. Then, before I wore one scanty bit of clothing or set foot on the stage, I woke to the reality that this wasn't a good idea for me. Sadly, in other times and situations, I have only come to the realization after the mistake was made.

Dorothy Goes Home

Years ago a stranger said to me, "You're like Dorothy in the Wizard of Oz. You made it all the way to Emerald City, but it's not what you expected it would be. You've seen through the sham and the imposter behind the curtain; you're disillusioned and now you're on a journey back home."

There couldn't have been truer words spoken into my life. I think we all are on this journey of remembering who we truly are. Like Dorothy, we've ventured out into the wild unknown, picking flowers along the way. But years pass, leaving us in a stupor of forgetfulness, needing intentional help and divine intervention to find our way home.

We can keep on going in the direction that betrays our hearts, or we can listen to Spirit reminding us of who we truly are. Can you hear it? Sometimes it's so faint that you must stop everything to take it in and get reacquainted. Sometimes a fall is the perfect setup to realign us and get us out of our stupor and awake again.

Perception Challenge and Exercise

Hey there, Dorothy! Been home lately? Have you bumped up against your own fickleness and imposter roles? Instead, lean into what you really feel and your at-homeness in your own skin.

Listen to that sweet whisper cluing you in on the truth, and lean into it.

Get excited! You're in for a personal revolution! Don't despise your double-mindedness in this moment. Acknowledge where you've been and how that's gotten you to this place. Congratulations! You're moving on and uncovering the truth.

When you discover your next fickle detour, celebrate that you're one step closer to congruence than you were previously. You'll not settle again for the same detour, but begin to recognize what resonates with you at the deepest level and what's a noisy, resounding gong.

Make a list of everything you dislike but have forced yourself into liking, and on the other side list everything you love. Take note of what you discover and begin to make room for the real, at-home-in-her-own-skin you!

Example List

- I don't do well in cubicles of grey and isolation.

- I don't thrive in big crowds of superficial pomp and circumstance.

- I can't handle the low energy of political maneuvering and corporate conspiring.

- I love color and passion, enthusiasm, inspiration and sunlight.

- I soar in settings of openness, deep conversation and small groups of friends, feasting on good food and wine where twinkly lights abound.

- Give me room to roam, explore and take in new sights and sounds so I can innovate, flow and communicate creatively.

Uprising! New Belief: Real uprising can only happen with the real you. If you're leaning hard into happiness, searching high and low, but you've left yourself out of the equation, it's a no-win proposition and it's time to regroup. It's not the real you!

You are the only person that gets to live your life, so if you've abdicated your life to others, you're not living it. Hello! What a wake-up call! Believe me, I've had wake-up calls more than once and continue to identify incongruences in my life.

Repeat out loud: I will awaken to my truest, me-est self. I will make space to listen and begin to remember who I truly am. I won't let the gaggle of flying monkeys hold me hostage to all means of do-gooding and performing while betraying my heart. I will awaken to my true song and laughter and celebrate their beauty. I am worth the celebration!

DAY 23: ABUNDANCE: WHY NOT NOW?

It's become gradually harder to discern the truth, making the landscape of the world even more tumultuous. Those we thought were reliable are exposed as liars, and those exposing lies and telling the truth are accused of falsehood. It seems many people have an agenda that does not include the public's wellbeing, but is instead focused on personal gain. This is not new; it's merely come to our attention more now that we live in the Internet Age.

What are we to believe when everyone is yelling "conspiracy"? Instead of being thrown about by every changing wind, we must hold firmly to the unchanging River of peace, hope and love that surrounds us, even more so in times of deceit.

Conspiracies

I know quite a few people who spent years talking about and nursing conspiracy theories. I'm not denying that there are plenty of conspiracies being hatched in the world, but have you noticed that what you focus on and what you truly believe you draw to yourself?

Although there is a difference between being an empowered truth teller and a victim, some of these individuals' greatest fears are confirmed because they draw the unjustness they're focusing on while spending hours and years talking about injustice. What happens next? They get to play the starring role of victim to the unjustness they perceived, nursed and expected to encounter. They get to say, "I told you so!" But wait a minute—was surrendering happiness and hope for the role of victim worth the exchange? I don't think so! Conspiracies, decay and the eroding of values we hold dear have been spoken of in every generation, but never as much as in the current climate, at least in my lifetime.

I want my life to remain hope-filled despite injustices in the world. I don't want to ignore them; I want to do my part to make the world a better place. However, I don't want to be so focused on injustice that I am suspicious and blinded to all that is good in the world. That means I take stock of what I perceive to be my own injustices.

- Am I blaming others for my relational difficulties or looking in the mirror at myself?

- Am I attracting the lack I expect to exist in my life, and if I am, will I take responsibility for the outcome or make changes to create something better?

Yep, Energy Attracts Energy

I'll say what I've said again: what we believe, whether we recognize it or not, will be drawn to us. We often wonder why a woman would return time and time again to domestic violence. The same question could be asked of why we return to our own negativity. What water supply are we drinking from, one of poverty or abundance, lack or faith?

We all struggle with negativity and must be intentional in redirecting it and choosing to think of things that are good and true and right. I would rather spend my energy believing the best and seeing the best in people, rather than focusing on the worst.

I would rather believe in generosity, grand gestures and possibility, rather than the converse. Nevertheless, I have to repeatedly make the choice to nurture and develop this practice instead of feeding on negativity. That means I have to recognize that there are circumstances I'm attracting without my intentional knowledge. I have to recognize when I am banking on the scarcity of a familiar, negative outcome.

As we begin to recognize our energy level, what we're attracting and where there continue to be blocks, those recognitions will show up in everything. Twice this week my yoga instructor spoke about exactly what I was experiencing and writing about. I wished I had been able to record it, because it was just so darn good!

Everywhere we turn, we are there! And so when I lay on my mat and felt Spirit opening my heart further, every part of my body responded and opened wider. Suddenly there was a firm nudge pressing my shoulders open deeper onto my mat, as the instructor hovered over me, intuitively highlighting what I was processing personally. I couldn't help but smile.

Parts of me have been hiding for a long time, parts that I perceived weren't palatable to others. As I open further and receive more into my being of who Love says that I am, I am able to stand taller, chest out and heart opened wider. My energy rises as I look inward instead of outward at the choir of opinion.

Today is short and sweet. We've all been in hiding, and now we can see ourselves in everything, abundance or scarcity. Everywhere we turn, we are there, and so is Love if we choose to engage it.

Perception Challenge and Exercise

Today, I invite you to take notice of your thoughts. Are you mulling over negative, defeatist thoughts, or are you supplying your brain and body with the energy of joy-inducing positivity?

If you find yourself stewing in negativity, simply ask for divine help to re-direct your thoughts. Open up your spirit to receive divine guidance that will fill your thoughts with peace, love and joy. There is no greater reality, truer path or more life-filling antidote. Choose joy and positivity today! Your attitude can alter the worst of circumstances by merely choosing hope and faith. Open your heart, stand tall and receive.

Uprising! New Belief: You're at a turning point. This is where you get to choose to let go of possibly years of rehearsing negative, energy-zapping thoughts. That means you're willing to let go of that story that's not work-ing for you and that same old line.

I have worked on retraining my brain and sending healing energy through-out my body to restore the nurturance and vitality that I neglected to give myself for years. Sure, I've eaten well and exercised, but more importantly, I'm no longer careless about the way my thoughts can counter all the good stuff I put in. I'm intentional with my thought life, although it is very much still a work in progress.

You too get to be proactive about the thoughts you probably never knew you were thinking. You get to pay attention to what's going on when your mood drops. You get to supplement your life with the necessary vitamins of good, positive, life-affirming thoughts—and challenge yourself when you don't believe them. This is a huge upgrade if you will take it. This is a chance for a true uprising!

Repeat out loud: There is always something to be joyful and thankful about, and so I will direct my thoughts in the way that I would have them go. I will let go of negativity as if it were being blown away by a strong, supportive wind. I will embrace the joy that is available in every moment and nurture a perspective that allows me to see little things for which I can be grateful. I choose the fullness of joy in the presence of God's Love for me moment by moment. That means living in the now, not in the fear of the future. What greater abundance is there?

DAY 24: NO MORE GRIDLOCK

The February 2009 issue of *Marie Claire* ran a story by Jan Goodwin entitled "Vigilantes in Pink." It told the story of a group of women living in the district of Banda, a remote rural area of India in which domestic abuse and political corruption is commonplace among the country's poorest citizens.

After learning that her good friend had been savagely beaten by her husband and was receiving continued indifference from the local police, Sampat Pal Devi, an outraged 47-year-old mother of five, organized dozens of her female neighbors and taught them how to fight back with sticks. Because of the pink saris these women chose to wear as a sign of their solidarity, they received the new name of the *Gulabi Gang*, or the "Pink Gang."

They have made such an impact that their work for justice is actually changing the landscape of the impoverished region, so much so that there are fewer rapes, more girls attending school, and now little need for violence in the name of self-defense.

This group has grown to number in the hundreds and is so popular that local stores can't keep up with the demand for pink saris! Just the mention of these local heroines incites fear in the heart of wannabe abusers, changing this little corner of the world as these women refuse to remain victims.

Although I am not suggesting violence as a strategy, I have to wonder if these women would still be alive had they passively accepted the brutality that was a way of life. Certainly they wouldn't have changed the face of a culture.

If we always do what we've always done, we'll always be the same. We don't have to settle for what is if we're bold enough to imagine what could be. Yet often, we determine we're stuck, as in gridlocked traffic, with no apparent way out.

What if the gridlock we imagine was simply the means to usher in a more expansive way of looking at our circumstance? What if the way out required action (Level 3 energy) and then the willingness to let go of what was keeping us stuck, so that we could rise to a more expansive Level 5 energy and onward?

Perception Challenge and Exercise

What if you looked differently at the thing in your life that feels like gridlock? What if you imagined a new open path or strategy before you? Imagine that the thing that hasn't worked and that you've always done previously suddenly gets new insight and revelation. This is what happens every time you are inspired with new possibility and ideas, so why not put it into regular practice? Why not open up to receive greater innovation, intuitive supply, resources and inspired ideas that take you out of stuckness and into newness?

Take that thing that seems unmovable and practice turning it on its head. First, begin by removing the judgment you've held toward yourself or another that continues to block you. Give yourself the kindness to move on into something new. Recognize that you are not a reflection of the thing that's been harming, trash-talking or blocking you, even if it's been you! You're so much more, and to receive more you have to be able to accept it! So try on the more. What actions do you need to take to get out of gridlock?

Uprising! New Belief: When you determine that you are more than the thing that is blocking you, you will become its worthy opponent, like the Pink Ladies who could have stayed in the worthlessness and defeat suggested by their abuse but instead rose up. I believe somewhere inside they determined that they had not been given a spirit of fear, but of power and love and a sound mind. They rose out of victimhood into a whole new definition of themselves, and with it a whole new day and life. Take hold of this strength and take it in. It is for you too as you move into a new belief and your own personal uprising. You are more than any defeat, ever!

Repeat out loud: Today I will begin to give thanks for all the new thoughts, inspired action and opportunities coming my way. I will walk out of the old and into the new expecting good things and believing that I am worth it. I will not stay in the defeat, but rise up into the promise and goodness of Love. I will receive Love in its multifaceted blessings and provisions in my life.

DAY 25: LEANING INTO FORGIVING OTHERS

We all have issues that cycle in and out of our life, those familiar pains we just can't seem to let go of. Thich Nhat Hanh said, "People have a hard time letting go of their suffering. Out of fear of the unknown, they prefer suffering that is familiar."

Sometimes our fear of the unknown keeps us tucked in with the pain we know. Sadly, we can nurture the toxic pain of unforgiveness, betrayal and rejection rather than face the risky, unknown territory within ourselves we need to address to let it all go.

It's hard to acknowledge that we have maligned others in the way others have maligned us. We haven't played fair and life isn't doled out fairly, with one exception: God is just. God is Love. And God loves every one of his children, even though we fail to comprehend the whole ball of wax concerning this mystery. God is not like us, and yet mysteriously, we are like him!

It is said that a sense of unworthiness lies at the root of all hate and those who cannot love feel a sense of unworthiness. The crazy thing is that God uses every fear, failure, injustice, ounce of negativity and sense of unworthiness to propel us forward. He uses our sin for our own wellbeing and redemptive purposes. Mind-blowing, isn't it?

Old, dead attachments can't be carried into the aliveness of the present, and so the more we live in the present, the more those resentments fade. God even uses old offenses to serve as compost of learning to produce richer soil in our lives.

The Cycle of Rebirth

Life is a cycle of death and rebirth, suffering and renewal, loss and restoration, over and over again, as pictured in the changing seasons. There is nothing alive that did not change to come into its present form.

Wintery bitterness and unmet expectations must be left behind to rise forth into springtime. As much as we might like the feel-good glow of springtime, we cannot bypass winter, but it's good to know that resurrection is always in the works. Spring never fails to appear.

This is the great paradox. Wrapped up within the looming pain of winter is the uncontainable, resurrecting Love of God. Beneath the euphoric melodies of springtime, Love carries with it sacrifice and suffering, and this is the paradox that makes our joy all the sweeter.

If you're a parent who has nursed a sick child, you know this reality of love to be true. Talk to someone experiencing the loss of a loved one, and you will see the very real pull of two worlds colliding, this one and the one veiled from our view. When our human heart, which mystically contains a seemingly uncontainable force, expands to acknowledge and recognize this goodness, an awakening and shift happens. It's impossible to remain the same!

Although we rarely recognize that we're tangled up in a redemptive process, just a few jaunts with awareness into unsolicited winters—be they rejection, betrayal or loss—and we begin to process the struggle differently. We can begin to take deeper breaths of rest and reprieve, reconnecting to life amidst the vast barrenness of winter, loosening our intent to escape or outrun the pain.

I think of winter as a season of cocooning or being safely tucked in amidst difficulty and darkness. Yet, like Dorothy in her detour in the poppy fields, the result is growth and forward movement. The ever-expanding spiral of life enlarges our capacity to awaken to Love and who we've been created to be as we recognize that everything God invites us into is good, even seasons of darkness.

We know that unless a grain of wheat falls into the ground and dies, it will never produce more wheat. And yet we protect ourselves from this process, thwarting the ultimate abundance and overflow of life that is coming and being formed in us. In this respect, winter is God's necessary and perfectly designed goodness.

Why is God's goodness so hard to remember when difficult circumstances challenge us? Why do we kick and flail when winter threatens to keep us hidden and forget that spring will reappear and that the things that are seen are made from that which is invisible? This joke says it all: "Why did the Buddhist coroner get fired? He kept marking the cause of death as 'birth.' "

There is always an unseen process before things are birthed and materialize. Giving way to flow with the process makes it all the more exciting.

Perception Challenge and Exercise

How can we begin to forgive others if we have not recognized the heaping goodness and forgiveness that have been granted to us? In our weakness, the Love of God is cultivating life from our darkness, and we discover that our limitation is no match for God's goodness. Unrivaled compassion for our suffering is met with tenderness and mercy toward our heartbreak and pain.

The ultimate paradox of the change agency of God, exchanging our sin for redemption and our pain for love, is mind-blowing and 100 percent contrary to our own scorekeeping bent. It is our resentment, malice, victimhood, negativity and all forms of catabolic energy that hinder and block the flow of this magnanimous River in our lives.

Instead of settling for the skewed lens of resentment and hurt, we can train our internal tuning fork to higher energy. We may have settled for a subpar reality, but we don't have to any longer! We can eclipse our pain and engage the "mind of Christ," where perfect Love casts out all fear. It's in this way that the gap is synced.

When I haven't quite crossed the bridge to forgiveness, I ask God for help. I ask that my heart would be able to receive forgiveness as I intentionally choose to forgive, despite my feelings. It's amazing, but every time I am willing to let go of ego and give up being right, I am guided across that bridge and invited into the present.

Take notice when you're hiding out and avoiding or refusing intimacy. There just may be unforgiveness lurking there. Even if there's been a situation that continues to threaten your safety and you've chosen to move away from an unhealthy relationship, you can still choose forgiveness; release your heart and the one you've held in contempt by leaving the past and experiencing the enveloping vastness of the present.

Uprising! New Belief: Congrats on releasing any bitterness you're holding because someone wouldn't meet your needs in the way you perceived necessary. Most people are doing the best that they can, and even when it doesn't appear to be so, forgiveness means that we take ourselves out of the role of judge and we recognize that everything in life serves as a teacher and mirror. Some things are smaller than they seem, and others, like the Love of God, are clearly more expansive than we can comprehend. Who are you to argue with reality? Let Love in!

Repeat out loud: I choose to upgrade my energy beyond the blame and victimhood connected to resentment. I choose to live at a higher frequency that doesn't steal my vitality and rob my life. I choose to forgive and release all those who have hurt or offended me. I choose to be free and happy in the present.

DAY 26: CRAVE MUCH?

Surely we've begun to notice the ways we often busy ourselves, refuse to sit still, dodge and employ all manner of techniques to avoid the things we're afraid of feeling, confronting or dealing with. Other times we crave what's "out there" and imagine if we obtain it we would be happier. To avoid and to crave are two different sides of the same coin; they're fear-driven forms of resistance that often keep us from taking responsibility or action.

Craving Is the Ultimate Drug

I am a natural visionary. I naturally see things that don't yet exist and work to create or establish them. Focus is also one of my top strengths, so I am able to accomplish a great deal or get 'er done! Although this can look quite proficient, productivity isn't necessarily the goal. There should instead be a balance of holding on and letting go.

Craving what we don't have is a powerful side-stepper. While staying in the feel-good space of dreaming about and craving what could be, we often avoid our present reality. Being adept at focusing and executing action steps could mean that we're merely busying ourselves to avoid what needs to be dealt with at a deeper level. Although we might employ astute skills to manifest what we crave, we could be winning at one game while losing at the game that truly matters.

Top Maneuvering Strategies

Avoidance magically closes our eyes to our current reality or situation while keeping us dancing around the thing we're afraid to see. In the end, craving is also avoidance. Yes, it's a double-sided coin. Both of these distractors, avoidance and craving. keep us cycling around the past of "what if" or looking ahead to "if only I had" while keeping us from facing our fears.

Acceptance Is Your Friend

Until we recognize our little song and dance, we're powerless to make changes. And honestly, we're powerless to recognize what the Spirit doesn't bring to our attention. However, now that you've been graced and gifted with the truth that I believe you have wanted on a deep level for some time, you're being led towards freedom.

Acceptance is always the first step for any rider in this rodeo. There is no way you can enter the ring, lasso the obstacle or take it down until you, my friend, have accepted that there is a better way. You must accept that:

1. You have something that needs to be lassoed, or better yet, you should just drop the rope and let 'er go.

2. You have divine strength and guidance supporting you, making you able to face the bull**** head on.

Right now there's a good chance that your heart is racing and your palms are sweating because of the thing you've been avoiding. You know this is your wake-up call. If this is the case, let out a big old "hallelujah!

"Remember, acceptance is the first step before you even pick up the lasso or mount the horse. Now, I don't recommend that you hang out here forever, creating another game of avoidance, but take a minute, breathe in acceptance and know that all you need to tackle your bull will be provided.

What got you to where you are now will not get you to where you want to go. It can't. To get somewhere different you must employ new strategy, breath and movement. Hey Dorothy, remember the path is already there and you're waking up to it now.

Perception Challenge and Exercise

Like me, you've probably employed a host of projects, ideas and sound, good ventures that weren't bad, but were merely occupying space so you could avoid deeper issues. You've given valuable time, energy and space to things that, in the end, truly don't matter.

You might have served on committees, joined groups, taken care of everyone else, created home improvement projects, engaged in empty relationships, watched way too much TV—the list of avoidance activities goes endlessly on.

Take stock and ponder the things that have served to keep you avoiding or craving a different reality than the one you presently know. Imagine that you can have a different reality.

If you are willing to sit in the empty space that initially feels foreign and out of place, you will be ushered into the most alive and truly "you" imaginable. This is the path.

Uprising! New Belief: What an amazing frontier you are crossing, one that most people never dare to venture into. You are discovering a more empowering life, way and self as you address all your avoidance and craving techniques and walk with them into acceptance. I can't help but feel like a proud mama or compatriot. Breathe in the freedom and glorious unhindered space awaiting you, filled with possibility and beauty.

Repeat out loud: I no longer need to hang out in avoidance and craving because I am learning to accept and welcome the open space in between where I am and where I'm going. I am learning to cowboy up and face my bull. I'm learning that there is so much more for me.

DAY 27: BREATHE IN SPACE

Interestingly, people can hold down a respectable job and look like they've got all the appropriate life skills but be severely lacking in emotional intelligence, health or relational capability. Children can't distinguish those who are fit from those who are unfit and usually mirror the examples presented to them. This is how uninvestigated patterns are passed down from one generation to the next.

We like to think we're highly independent individuals making our own choices. Yet how often do we recognize that we haven't chosen at all, but life is reflecting back to us what we have taken into us? Life mirrors and reflects itself time and time again.

Jane Austen's *Pride and Prejudice* portrays this well, and for that reason it is one of my daughter's and my favorites. If you haven't read it or seen the movie, I highly recommend it. It's filled with a cast of eccentric, manipulative, immature and good-hearted people who illustrate how life mirrors our deepest perceptions.

Although Lizzie and Mr. Darcy initially judge and project onto each other their own prejudice and arrogance, in time they move past their own limitations, as well as the limitations of those surrounding them, to find love, but not before time apart and seasons of reflection.

Crumbly Portions and Relational Ghosts

Early in the book, I wrote about anorexia showing up in many facets of my life, particularly the starvation of love. If you're like me, you've often settled for the crumbs in your life.

I believe this tendency starts early, when caregivers either don't know how or are emotionally unable to show healthy love for a variety of reasons. In my case, there was mental illness and an inability to love or parent healthily.

My reaction to withheld love was to withhold it from myself. Hence the many ways of starving myself. Those that don't have it withhold it in one way or another. In coaching this is referred to as "moving toward" or "moving against," and it's something we'll explore further later in the week.

It's only when we choose to nurture our lives that we begin to grow healthier. This is true whether we have been emaciated or, on the flip side, bloated and overstuffed with all of life's compensations.

Part of becoming healthy is refusing to settle for the crumbs of relationships. Owning and valuing our worth means we let go of partnering with others who fail to value us, because we've learned to value ourselves. Being alone in a relationship that is merely occupied by a space holder is actually more painful than merely choosing to be alone.

As we begin to care for ourselves, it prepares us to choose mutually healthy relationships where both parties are present and able to show up to the table. No shift in relational dynamics can happen until we recognize our own incongruences and learn to care for ourselves in a healthy manner.

Healthy relationships start with us. We need to get comfortable with the empty space that is reserved for our growth, self-care and divine inner being, rather than filling our lives with space holders. Choosing to intentionally breathe in space to nurture health and wholeness is necessary.

Perception Challenge and Exercise

Healthy relationships begin on the inside, where we learn to feed on love rather than settle for malnourishment. Letting go of space holders is a sign of growth, honor and self-respect. It is also a profound step in dealing with the double-mindedness of playing nice to the crowd while being dishonest with ourself.

Take some time and jot down the space holders that you need to release. Welcome the emptiness that you've previously filled through busyness and unhealthy means.

There is nothing out there that will satisfy unless your insides have first been nurtured. There is no better meal, handcrafted cocktail, vacation or ultimate intoxication than awakening to the Love within you. Until this is nurtured, space holders will leave you unsatisfied. So be selfish with your own portion. Take the time to drink in love for yourself.

Uprising! New Belief: At times it's hard to swim against the current, to sit out while others are running, to quiet oneself in the midst of a frenetic storm, but it's the kindest kindness you can give yourself. I applaud your bravery to stop the merry-go-round and make changes in this way. This leads to personal health, growth and a rising up of new proportions. Don't grow weary in doing this good for yourself that, in time, will be felt not only within, but in your relationships with others.

Repeat out loud: I am worth the investment of pulling aside for realignment and nurturance. My relationship to myself is the most important relationship in my life. I choose to follow the leading of the Spirit to guide me into healthy, affirming, life-giving relationships with God, others and myself. This is the ultimate self-care.

DAY 28: UPRISING: MOVING TOWARDS LIFE

It's been said that we can safely assume we've created God in our own image when we think God hates all the same people we do.

Energy such as hatred is toxic. As a professional coach, I work with clients using my training in advanced communication skills to help them improve the energy they bring to their lives. Brené Brown also helped introduce the world to one way we use energy in her theory of "moving toward" or "moving away or against."[14]

It's not hard to sense the different energy in "moving towards" versus "moving away or against" simply from the words. When we're opposing something, there's a sense of dread and fear, even panic, that wants to move in the opposite direction. And when we're unclear about this internally, it presents as the incongruence we've previously discussed, or an internal tug of war.

When we perceive something as holding us back, it elicits a reactionary response that reeks of negativity rather than positive energy. And as we know, the energy of "moving away" is taxing on our bodies and spirits.

Think of how this energy shows up at work or in relationships. There's a sense of drudgery that requires powering through with willfulness and even the need for major amounts of caffeine. There is a substantial amount of duty and force that comes with this energy that isn't sustainable over the long haul. Sadly, I think some people would rather get sick than get

---

14   Brené Brown, *Rising Strong* (New York: Spiegel & Grau, 2015).

honest with themselves.

This isn't to say that life should always be unicorns and endless parades with candy and presents. We actually need conflict that causes us to bump up against the falsehoods we hold so we can grow and realign. Identifying the energy we bring to our life reveals much about our motives, who we're playing to and our outlook. Learning to shift our energy changes environments and outlooks, such as a job that is less than ideal. We not only can find happiness amidst the difficult or mundane, we can open up to avenues we may have never seen before.

It's Always About Energy

Imagine the energy of moving or running towards something or life in general. This energy carries a sense of longing, delight, anticipation and excitement, as if we're running toward a lover we've glimpsed in the distance. There's no hesitation, only openness.

We can feel this radiating from people, just as we can also feel the toxicity of the opposite. Our bodies and our lives feel the energy of "moving toward" each day in anticipation, or the negativity and the low energy of dread.

How many of us spend large allotments of our energy on "moving away" instead of "moving towards"? How often do we have our guard up to protect us from something we've outrun in the past or fear in the future? Honestly, I don't know if I've met anyone that doesn't exhibit this frailty, because if we've ever been hurt we've stood in this posture.

There was a time I worked hard to keep my fists up high. Because my new freedom felt wobbly, I worked hard to protect myself from the abuse that I would no longer tolerate. Yet the truth is, it's much more powerful to "move toward" the things we are for rather than against what we dislike.

Sadly, our egos love to rant but fail to recognize the frailty in ourselves that we attack in others. Coming from the spirit of truth and love, we're able to connect with a world that may see things quite differently because we recognize that our own shortcomings are equal to those of our brothers or sisters. It's only from this posture of humility and "moving toward" that the world will ever truly change.

Maybe that is why God said, "Eat what is good, and let your soul delight itself in abundance" (Isaiah 55:2, NJKV). Feed on fear, hate and all forms of toxic energy, or feed on what is good and releases delight and abundance even in difficult times. We get to choose the kind of energy we want to release into the world. We get to choose if we want to sow more pain or hope.

Perception Challenge and Exercise

When Spirit reveals the toxic energy of "moving away or against," you have an opportunity to choose your response. Positive energy will open you up to flow effortlessly in the atmosphere of life-giving love, while resisting and "moving against" will shut you down.

Through Spirit you can find the deep, resounding pulse of your yeses and the free-spirited and untethered openness of "moving toward," rather than the judgment and resistance of "moving against or away."

The beauty of "moving toward" is that it gives you the ability to stay in your own lane without needing to be identified with anything other than being a child of God. From this posture you can be free from ego's need to defend, deflect and "move against." You can stand in love, for love, and watch it shift the fear, rage and confusion of those around you. Honestly, sometimes it causes confusion in those who live from a dualistic reality.

Identify where the energy of "moving away or against" shows up in your life. Where do you need to shift your energy forward in a new direction?

Uprising! New Belief: The discovery of all the ghost relationships, space holders, avoidance techniques and "moving away from and against" energy we've looked at this week makes me excited! I picture your wings getting lighter and stretching out with a new resurgence of life that's coming to you. You're getting ready to fly. It's a good day to be alive!

Repeat out loud: There is no need to resist what happened in the past because it is done and gone. There is no need to jump on the bandwagon of pain, confusion and anger that often surrounds me. I can choose what I feed on. I carry the power to move forward into love and no longer need the safety of the past or the spiral of the low energy and drama around me. Today I get to practice "moving toward" in life through hope and love. I come with wide-open willingness.

PART II:

It's Not What We Know, It's What We Can't Comprehend

In Part I, we talked about how our perception affects our lives. In Part II, we will continue this vein but dive deeper into the mystery of what is beyond our comprehension. We will explore the mysterious and unfathomable goodness of the Love that surrounds us and how awakening to this Presence transforms us. We will carry the awareness of our default settings that we talked about in Part I into an opportunity for a greater consciousness expansion throughout Part II.

WEEK 5:

Engaging with Mystery

Day 29: Indispensable to Our Happiness

Day 30: Spirit, Mystery and Love

Day 31: Wilder Love

Day 32: Currencies and the Dance

Day 33: God Paints with a Broader Stroke

Day 34: Breathe In the Ultimate Intoxication

Day 35: Uprising: What You Seek Is Seeking You

INTRODUCTION TO WEEK 5

Engaging with Mystery

For me, 2016 started off with the word *giddy*. It resonated strongly through my being, as if it was my schoolyard playground of learning for the year. It seemed particularly poignant after the recent passing of my mother that this book about happiness was birthed. Without thought, this book about happiness was birthed. I love the way God thinks and introduces new territory in our lives.

In 2016 it seemed as if the seeds of ten years of wintering finally broke forth. New revelation seemed to fall off the tree and into my life as fat, plump fruit, continuing to challenge and shift my ability to receive greater joy and giddiness.

The year 2017 began with the same sense of foreknowing of what was being initiated for the new year. The word I received was *presence*, and it ushered in a resounding wallop, fully delivering on its promise.

As we move into the final two weeks of *Uprising*, we're going to explore more of the mysterious doorway that carries us beyond ourselves into the supernatural and mysterious waters of God's presence and the intoxicating fruits of peace and joy that accompany it. Talk about mysterious! Buckle up for the ride!

DAY 29: INDISPENSABLE TO OUR HAPPINESS

In the movie *Becoming Jane*, the character Lady Gresham, speaking of her nephew, says, "Wesley is indispensable to my happiness." And there is one thing that is utterly indispensable to our happiness. Let me explain.

Some people deny the reality of God, yet we all have gods in our lives, whether we recognize them or not. We might even profess to believe in and worship God while our thoughts and beliefs are more accurately centered on fear, scarcity and resistance, far below a reality of faith or belief in God. This is a challenging proposition. Do we truly believe what we think we believe, or are we fooling ourselves?

Surely by now it's not hard to concede that we become what we give ourselves to. We become the thing we focus on or, one could say, "worship." When we spend our energy feeding on negativity, it oozes out of every cell. When we feed on life and love, we resonate and radiate from a higher present reality.

I am challenged by this notion and you should be too, because I frequently witness the divide between what I think I believe and the varying reality manifesting in my life. However, recognizing the gap is a profoundly good place to be. It reveals that there is a greater truth calling us forward that we've yet to recognize.

Rather than reducing God to our own limited perspective, a willingness to move beyond our current experience opens us up to new contexts outside of our own affectations, familiarities or personal and cultural "speak." We have the opportunity to have the divine nature of God revealed in and to us. What an exciting notion! Anticipation and expectation open the channel to receive.

Take a moment to ponder how marvelous it is that we're not alone, flailing about in our own notion of independence. An all-knowing, all-foreseeing Creator intimately engages with and directs the lives of the children he created. As we've discussed, some fail to recognize this intimate connection and live as orphans. Living in this way alters what is available to us. The question is, will we receive all that is available to us?

It's in Our DNA

Imagine if we tried to bypass the reality that we came into the world through our mother. No extenuating circumstance can alter the fact that she existed and we're intertwined with her. How much truer could this be of the Creator God?

Awakening to this realization is a milestone in any life, when we suddenly recognize that there was a plan and we are part of God's delight. This awakening is like coming home for Christmas where the table is set, the meal is prepared and we're suddenly wrapped up in the middle of the surrounding love.

Imagine suddenly being so awakened that we could recall what transpired as we were formed in the heart of God and in our mother's womb. Although we may not remember when God imagined and created us or being inside the womb of our mother, we can experience the reality of God's heart for us.

Utterly Indispensable to Your Happiness

I have no stake in others believing exactly what I believe, except to the extent that I know there is no happiness apart from discovering our eternal self. This is our truest sense of home and our truest identity. There is no possible way to bypass home and still be at home in ourselves.

Although many would deny the suggestion that they're living as if cut off, thirsty or malnourished, yet all the while lives and relationships testify to that. What if we could awaken and return to our innately supplied happiness? Returning to Source and home to our truest nature is like discovering an untainted river amidst drought on every side. We are free to drink and be satiated.

This drink is profoundly different from all the other drinks available. For instance, drinking fruit punch that initially seems pleasing to the palate will in the end leave a terrible aftertaste and greater thirst for pure water. We might temporarily get full, but in truth we're merely bloated and not satisfied or nurtured. Without really tasting the goodness of pure water, we don't know what we're missing. There is one thing indispensable to our life and true happiness, and that is the pure drink of the fountain that is God.

Through the remainder of the book we will explore this unimaginable, indescribable Life that is indispensable to our happiness and rediscover the pure drink that fills the gaping hole.

Perception Challenge and Exercise

Today you have the opportunity to check in and determine if there is a gaping hole that is separating you from happiness. Are you standing on the outside looking in when you are meant to experience a fully loved identity?

You can move forward in your day and your life from two profoundly different energies and beliefs. One requires nothing; you just keep moving along as you always have, treading water. The other requires faith. It requires diving headlong into the River and lapping up the refreshing drink because you choose to believe that before time began you've been seen and known and loved. You were created and fashioned in Love from the heart of God.

The amazing thing is that everything you need for faith and believing has been supplied. It is within you. There has always been and always will be ample love and support for you.

All it takes is willingness to let the Spirit awaken and expand within you. The Spirit is the life energy that will teach you the way to go and help you get in step as you cultivate relationship and strength from within.

Today you get to choose to exercise a faith muscle that goes against your rational mind, which wants to focus on the negative, circumstantial lack in the world. Instead, you can choose an eternal and unchanging reality: God's Love for you.

Challenge your scarcity and fear by choosing to feast on all things life-giving and affirming, swinging wide into hope, love and joy. See if lingering residuals from your scorched wasteland begin to turn into an inner oasis where you are more than satisfied.

When we fall into fear, we have surrendered our trust and faith and merely need to recalibrate our perception and return to love. This means trusting in a Higher Power that exceeds our present circumstance. Invite the Spirit to lead you into a Love journey that awakens you to the ultimate Love and homecoming.

Uprising! New Belief: Any feeling of lack or idea of hiding out, distancing ourselves or withholding love only reveals that we are parched and thirsty and need to drink again from the right water supply. People are not our source, period. We're supplied from a much greater well. Choosing to believe is the biggest internal uprising of all!

Repeat out loud: I believe in divine Love that has always upheld me, even though I have failed to recognize it at times. I believe that there is no separation between this Love supply and me. I will continue to let love enlarge itself in me and cultivate a lens that is perpetually turned toward the sunshine of love and the River supply that never runs dry. I believe that I am fully encompassed in love. It is this love that defines me through and through. I will feast and saturate myself on God's kindness so that it overflows into my relationships, my life and how I view myself. I believe in and am awakening to the Love that surrounds me and is indispensable to my life.

DAY 30: SPIRIT, MYSTERY AND LOVE

There are no words to describe God without plenty of conjecture and speculation. How could we truly know the Source of transcendence?

In *The World As It Is*, Chris Hedges says, "All of us find God not in what we know, but in what we cannot comprehend."[15] It's there in this *unknowing* that we're taken into the River called Presence, an oasis in the desert, a door to true happiness in our lives and a means to transformation.

Our "knowing"—our rational mind and need for control—interfere with learning, growth and Spirit's experiential flow. It's comparable to trying to train a teenager who thinks they know more than we do, when in reality their knowledge is limited. We are the proverbial teenager.

Our conviction in our "knowing" creates distance and forfeits the grace necessary to humble ourselves. I am baffled by the times I've pressed my way through the dense fog of confusion, as if struggling alone. Why would I think that was necessary? Why would I be so foolish? The presence of God is available, but often I'm too dulled to recognize it.

Spirit, Not Head

As I mentioned, the word *presence* resounded in my Spirit leading up to and through the commencement of the new year. It was like a clean breath of oxygen filling my lungs. It was like a refreshing dip into a mountain stream where I encountered the thick Presence of God anew. It's as if I

15   Chris Hedges, *The World As It Is* (New York: Nation Books, 2001), 10.

was escorted into the Secret Garden, overladen with fragrant blossoms and golden sunshine.

This was not something I expended effort to make happen but sublimely found myself in, so that all I could do was float on my back in ease. If this sounds like some hippy experience, it might as well be (without the drugs). The thick intoxication of the depths of God's Love is by far the best wine. However, we have to be willing to give up our uptight posture of Sunday-school hands neatly folded in our lap and engage in this splendor over propriety.

Personally I think of God as a Trinitarian bundle, three parts of mystical completeness profoundly more mystical and unusual than our little heads can comprehend. The thing is, the comprehending doesn't happen in our heads. It's a spirit-to-spirit connection, and that's why we're so baffled by all the mystery wrapped up inside this Mystery.

We're made in the image of a Spirit Being. We are a *Being*, not a *Doing*. You can only *be* in Spirit; you can't get there through effort. Spirit is a "now" person, not a "was" or "will be" person, although Spirit is enduring and without end. Spirit is like breath. It can't be captured for later, only experienced now, so whenever we resist the now, we're resisting the Spirit.

Let me feebly attempt to illustrate what can't be communicated with words. When we tell a story from our heart, communicating things we're passionate about or understand well, the words flow out as if they're alive. The listeners are taken in with us into the moment, as if the words breathed are spontaneous moving energy, like the wind that can't be corralled or music floating in the atmosphere.

Conversely, should we look down and refer to our notes, it's easy to leave the experiential present and enter into the logic center of our brain where we control and force a direction. Should the listener suddenly recall a to-do list, they too have wandered from the present Presence into the future or past.

This happens all day long as we move in and out of the present moment. Sadly, some of us rarely inhabit the present but are stuck in the past or fearing and anticipating the future, and as a result we are rattled with anxiety. Imagine the stress this creates when we're anywhere besides where we are in the moment.

Neither logic, knowledge nor ego are experiential or present tense. Ego observes and judges. It never functions in the present tense, but leaves the moment to operate from the outside looking in.

We can actually bring awareness to the way our bodies and minds shift out of openness and revert to being constricted and controlled when we move out of experiencing the present moment. Similarly, the breath of God's presence is in the moment. When we're in the present, there's no outside looking in, although Spirit can impart a kind of present-tense revelation or foreseeing that mystically reveals the "mind of Christ" in the moment. This is entirely different from ego's outside-looking-in stance of judging and viewing life from past triggers and experiences. Spirit takes us into an otherworldly experience if we are open to encountering it.

Spirit Meets Us in Our Unknowing

If we could step outside our linear perspectives and move into the expansiveness of Spirit, we'd see that the journey is riddled with mystery and beauty. When in the Spirit, even the twisted jabs of pain or the murky waters of darkness can be doused with exuberant intoxication. Our Spirit already knows God, because Spirit knows Itself, and Spirit calls to Spirit in us.

The awakened soul recognizes the flow of divine Love and the indwelling Spirit within as the return to paradise. It's an intoxication that is unexplainable and otherworldly, an experience that mystics of old have talked of and all of the sages of earth cannot explain away. It experientially does to the senses what drug addicts are in search of.

In the book *Feel*, Matthew Elliott tell us that because much of Western church culture has stressed what not to feel or how to feel, rejecting any sort of emotional outlet, we will find other things to get intoxicated on. "We must find our emotional outlet somewhere. Sometimes, I think the reason people get addicted to stuff is because they have worked so hard not to feel the things they were made to feel and enjoy."[16]

One of the most common methods for rejecting our human, emotional makeup—putting head before heart—goes back to the picture of the Garden of Eden and the two profoundly different trees there. Whether you believe this story to be truth or myth, look closer for what it reveals.

A Return to the Garden

In the Garden, God told Adam and Eve never to eat from the Tree of the Knowledge of Good and Evil. Doing so would keep them living under the

[16] Matthew Elliott, *Feel* (Oxford: Monarch Books, 2008), 38.

legal ramifications of the law, which never satisfies. The law provides the appearance of knowing what is good and evil through a grab at Godlikeness. What Adam and Eve failed to understand was that Godlikeness was something they already possessed. Humans are made in the image of God.

Conversely, The Tree of Life spoke of that which surpassed humanity's sense of knowing and moved into an entirely different and otherworldly realm beyond the law of good and evil. Jesus is the picture of the fruit of this tree that provides unending life and perpetual feasting far beyond what human understanding can obtain.

Eve saw the fruit and surmised that it was good, but after eating from the Tree of Knowledge, Adam and Eve felt naked, ashamed and exposed. Losing a true sense of who they were and where they'd come from set the course for humanity to stumble. We mistakenly surmise that reality equates to the evidence of tangibles and the appearance of what seems to be good in our own eyes.

This trap is the antithesis of faith, which is an open posture poised to receive. Settling for Tree Number Two and its measly crumbs of human knowledge of right and wrong is the ultimate limitation and blindness that keeps us hiding, covered in shame and destined to decay.

Because God's Love is so great for humankind, he made a way for us to return to the life intended for us and the truth of who we really are. The Father provided his Son, Jesus, the bridge that took upon himself the sin and blindness of all humanity. Jesus is the Tree of Life, and through relationship with him we can experience unending eternal life in paradise.

The whole tree story's significance, its redemption of humanity's poor choice, is utterly beautiful. Christ—the bridge to life and the answer to the blindness of settling for separation, a mere code of ethics and warring for what's already been freely given to us—is simply mesmerizing. This is romance at its best and the greatest love story that ever was.

The great awakening is to understand that we've been woven into this eternal relationship with the Trinity, as Jesus stepped in on our behalf. Christ's crucifixion for humanity's sin means that we're no longer separate individuals.

We were nailed to the cross with our sin, were buried, died and mystically rose again into newness of life with Christ. The old Tree-of-Knowledge person died and was replaced by a Life-in-Christ person that lives forever. This means we can live far above the limitations of knowledge and experience life now and forever!

What was broken couldn't be fixed; it had to be entirely replaced, like a worn-out garment whose patches could no longer hold together. The seductive knowledge the tree offered couldn't produce life.

Perception Challenge and Exercise

Whether or not you believe this, hopefully you can see how the low energy of living from your head is an antithesis to the Life Source that surpasses your understanding. Truthfully, knowledge can never intoxicate us but, like that old tree in the Garden, will merely wither and die.

Here's the truth, should you choose to accept it: the old you is no longer a fit. You've been dragging the dead, lifeless carcass around while trying to swat it out of the way. Yet the struggle is completely in vain. You have to let it go and be done with it because the old you is dead and no longer exists. You have been replaced!

You are not a mixture of good and evil. The flesh has been killed. It's dead! You possess the life of Christ, so you must put away the double-minded behavior. It's entirely a myth that you must overcome the flesh or war against the devil sitting on one shoulder.

Often people talk about a process of "becoming holy" using the term *sanctification*. This is possibly one of the biggest hindrances to accepting the freedom that is yours to possess. The idea of working for it utterly flies in the face of it, making it impotent. Sanctification is not a process but a person. Any attempt to make yourself good is an affront to the goodness that you now are because of Jesus, the bringer of life. If you should momentarily have poor judgment, simply return to the truth of who you are. Sound too easy? That's the grace that's been supplied. You can't work for it! That's the beauty of the Gospel.

This is not a do-it-yourself self-help program. It takes faith to believe it in the first place! Søren Kierkegaard said, "There are two ways to be fooled. One is to be believe what isn't true; the other is to refuse to believe what is true."

Uprising! New Belief: Even if this seems ridiculous or far too mystical and mind-blowing to comprehend (and it is), why would you turn down the gift? Why would you let your sense of "knowing" rob you of something that exceeds your comprehension? Why would you settle for the old when you have been given the brand new upgrade extraordinaire?

Repeat out loud: If I am confounded by the utter expansiveness of God, I'm in a good place. God is much too wonderful to place inside a limited box. Knowledge will never provide the power for transformation that God has already secured. I will stand in the mind-blowing, good-news reality through faith in a God that secured my life and freedom. And yes, I choose to believe and ask for God's faith to believe what I cannot really comprehend. He has me right where he wants me and I will rest in that security.

DAY 31: **WILDER LOVE**

Most of the women I know look like they have it all together. However, this doesn't by any means reveal that they actually do—they just *look* like they do.

In my family of origin (as in many), the appearance of "good" reigned supreme. This didn't actually mean that things were good, but they appeared to be so and continued to roll on in this manner.

While living under this same pattern of things "appearing good," my mom also resisted the confinement it created. Through her lifestyle of frequent moves, travel and out-of-the-norm thinking for her era, she ousted the appearance of the appropriate or good, particularly when her teen pregnancy sliced a gaping hole in the illusion.

As a child needing stability, when my mom swung hard against restraint, I swung to brace myself for the next big upheaval my gypsy momma would surprise us with. I worked to maintain a sense of control and the appearance that all was good in our out-of-control world. Sadly, my misguided overcorrection is the same one that has plagued humanity since the Garden and caused us much heartache and a propensity to gravitate toward and align with the *illusion* of good. That's why we've settled for the appearance of the perfect Martha Stewart, all-things-in-order world. We've traded life for an illusion.

We trade in real sustenance for the illusion that appears to be good and right. Having been seduced by a form of rightness that is a direct antithesis of true life, we don't even recognize the downgrade. That illusion is like a vampire sucking the life out of us until we're so completely undone and drained of life that we're actually positioned to encounter the real rather than the mere appearance of it!

The Real

Whatever you believe about God, I hope you believe God to be enduring, eternal, all-loving, life-giving and good, as opposed to a deity with a whip in his hand. I hope you believe God is good, passionate and head-over-heels intoxicated with you.

Ever since the Garden, we've been caught up in the rat race of chasing after inconsequential lovers instead of being swept up into the Love that resounds within our being. We've traded in intoxication, life and passion for far lesser lovers.

Think about it: enduring intoxication could only ever come from the life that is wrapped up in God because that life never withers, fades or ends! That life is breathed through a passionate love affair with humanity.

But we have exchanged a love affair with God for the long-distance sur- veillance of spectators, while daily pounding out our desire to "know" in- stead of *experience* the mystery and intoxication of intimate relationship.

Loving and falling in love are experiences. Intimacy and relationship are always in the present tense because they are always experiential. Although there might be tangible markers in our memories of a place and circum- stance related to love, what lingers is the feeling of the experience. That's what we hope never fades. That's what we dream of. Yet we don't know that what we are dreaming of is a distant memory of the Garden from before we settled for illusion. We don't know that Someone is dreaming of and longing for us and our return to love.

John Mark McMillan wrote in his poignant song "Wilderlove," "So what have we become / Just pedestrian / There is no domestic heart."[17]

Having exchanged relationship and the fullness of life and passion for an illusion, we have attempted to domesticate the heart, which by its very nature cannot be domesticated; it's meant to be wild and passionate. Ever tried not to be in love with someone? We can't tell our hearts whom to love. Sure, we can shut them down or compartmentalize our feelings and life, but in truth the heart can't be domesticated.

Plenty of people try to enter into a lifeless business agreement in marriage and with God. A legal relationship could be called cold, institutional and distant. Where there is no real engagement, there is no intimacy, just formula. You can't be intimate from a safe distance.

Imagine how a lover's expression of love that is trite, memorized or read from a Hallmark card reeks of inauthenticity and lack of depth. That's because clichés fail to intoxicate; they're not present tense.

People entrenched in the use of clichés, or using only the appropriate cultural language of any tribe, exhibit an attachment to their human understanding, laws and rules (Tree of Knowledge) and lack the pulsating, vibrant, authentic reality of the Tree of Life.

17   John Mark McMillan, "Wilderlove," August 12, 2016, Lionhawk Records.

Real love, not lust, is otherworldly because it's birthed and breathed of God.

It exudes the sloppiness of a lingering kiss, the unpolished and sponta-neous present moment that is risky and mysterious and takes us into something beyond ourselves. It's the act of giving it all in a willingness to dive off the high board into the mysterious, wild waters of "Wilder Love." If this seems foreign to us, we aren't experiencing it.

There is a place for knowledge. I've certainly written about and offered up knowledge and wisdom that have equipped my clients and me for life. We need to recognize our behavior, but we also need to understand that there is something entirely higher than human wisdom or behavior. Spirit is the guide that takes us into the realm of Wilder Love's supernatural trans-formation and life. There is a word for anyone that would settle for the impotence of human wisdom over divine: *fool*. Yet we all are fools plenty of the time.

There's no better way to describe the mysterious intoxication of God's Presence and Love than this verse: "They are abundantly satisfied with the fullness of your house; and you give them drink from the river of your pleasures. For with you is the fountain of life; in your light we see light" (Psalm 36:8–9, NKJV).

C. S. Lewis is said to have said, "Discovery is the vocation of children." I would say falling in love is nothing short of a return to our childlike, first-breathed heart. We must become like little children again to enjoy and engage in the mystery of the unknown. Truth be told, all apathy or de-spondency in our life shows signs of lack of intimacy and failure to engage in relationship with the mystery of divine Love.

Isn't fascination with mystery why space exploration began? Isn't it why we sent rockets to the moon to discover unknown frontiers? We are hungry for the mystery that is God. This hunger is actually God hungering to be known in us. And God's Presence is what makes us come alive to him, not our attempts to figure it out, get smart or hustle. It's engaging with mystery.

Albert Einstein said, "The most beautiful thing we can experience is the mysterious. It is the source of all true art and all science. He to whom this emotion is a stranger, who can no longer pause to wonder and stand rapt in awe, is as good as dead; his eyes are closed."[18]

Perception Challenge and Exercise

How much do you engage with mystery? Do you find yourself needing finite answers, definitive understanding and planned agendas? Missing the love?

Someday, when you look back over your life, you will remember experiences and feelings of love toward and from the people who touched your life. Love will be your measure and final destination. The things you *think* are important in this fleeting moment will fade and be immaterial.

Enjoy the journey without thinking about the destination. Move into the expanse of Spirit and the flow of the River. Move into the unwinding mystery of relationship with Holy Spirit and the Trinitarian Bundle. Open yourself up to Wilder Love.

18   Albert Einstein, in *Living Philosophies: A Series of Intimate Credos*
        (New York: Simon and Schuster, 1931).

How do you begin? Invite God, the Father, Son and Spirit, to lead you into the expansiveness of a Love relationship. It's that simple.

Uprising! New Belief: There is no greater destination than Love. There is no greater route than Love. Oh, what a journey you are on. It will result in a beautiful destination, but if you merely focus on the destination, you will entirely miss the majesty available right now in a present-moment relationship. You are rising up to your most alive self as you engage with the Love of God.

Repeat out loud: I came from Love and will return there. I am a Spirit being, so I will give attention to my spirit. I will cultivate the biggest part of myself that I've often neglected. I will listen for the flashing beacon of home as Spirit leads me, because I am becoming more aware of the present moment and all that is alive for me. I am feasting from the Tree of Life and the River of Presence.

DAY 32: CURRENCIES AND THE DANCE

We like to think that God is like us, though our version of God is entirely slanted, nonexistent or hilariously small. We fight hard to prove that he'll quit on us, give up or walk away and that his Love *is* conditional. We self-sabotage by letting our circumstances declare that we just aren't lovable. Meanwhile he stands with open arms saying, "There's so much Love for you here. It's freely given and you don't have to prove yourself to me. You are utterly safe and protected from shame because in my Love there is no accusation or judgment. You can't earn my Love and you can never lose it."

Yet, in a cocky, grown-up stance, we roll our eyes at the mystery of Love. We philosophize and pontificate while human wisdom, man-made laws, opinions, knowledge and reasoning will always fail us through their utter limitation. I believe they're meant to fail so we can experience that which supersedes them.

Thankfully, God mysteriously tracks us down like a lover that will not be branded indifferent or abusive, outsmarting the antagonist within us and causing us to show our hand and throw down our obviously deflated chips for a currency that is always elevated. There is just no way to lose with God's currency. It's all been rigged in our favor!

Currencies

Do you realize that the world is made up of currencies, or the things we spend to purchase something, our buying power? Think about the currency we're using.

What are we spending our life on? Is the currency calculated? Are we buying and trading our life through pleasing and performing with a placating curtsy?

Are we living in the safe and calculated sphere of work or relationships so that we can detach from any threat of truly revealing ourselves and growing in depth and intimacy? Our choices can be very costly as we spend our dignity, self-worth and ultimately our life purchasing an idea of security that in the end might not be substantiated.

Yet many live by measuring calculated risks that affect the bottom line. Sadly, choosing a life that merely looks good on paper fails to intoxicate. There's no romance in the calculated maneuvering that causes us to lose the passion and wonder that once had us gazing at the moonlight and pulling aside to discover new vantage points along the way. And I'm sure we could agree that there is no dance partner that wants to be considered a good, calculated risk.

Duty and Booty Calls

I suspect the reason that this generation fears intimacy, needs control and calculates risks is because they have lost the mystery of romance. This has skyrocketed the "booty call" into preeminence. You're probably familiar with the term, which refers to a late-night call to hook up for sex. It's unpleasant to receive a booty call when you're hoping for romance and relationship. Receiving a "duty call" is just as unpleasant.

A duty call is when you realize the caller is lacking heart or true interest in you, romantic or otherwise. You surmise through the tone of the caller that you're merely a box to be checked off a to-do list that soothes someone's conscience. It never feels good to be played rather than truly engaged. Although we might try to convince ourselves otherwise, a duty call is as empty as a booty call.

Jesus never encouraged feigned enthusiasm, heartless prayer or acts of insincere and artificial adoration. In fact, inspired by the Spirit, King David prayed, "Search me, O God, and know my heart! Try me and know my anxious thoughts; and see if there be any hurtful way in me, and lead me in the everlasting way" (Psalm 139:23–24, NASB).

The Dance

We all truly want to engage in romance, which is to engage in the mysterious, experiential and powerfully intoxicating cadence of the dance. The magnetic pull of romance on our heartstrings is Spirit breathing, revealing and proclaiming Christ's existence and love in us and all around.

Furthermore, to actually engage in romance and fall in love, we have to be willing to let go of our ideas about someone and walk with uncertainty into the curiosity of discovery. That's the thrill of falling in love and the joy of the dance. It might look like unreliable currency, but its dividends are without measure. It's why wide-eyed lovers are willing to bet it all on love. It's usually our fear and need for control that blocks love in our life.

In the end we spend our currency through two avenues, fear or faith, and both carry the feeling of uncertainty. While fear is a narrowing, toxic and suffocating presence that provides no advantage, faith reaches beyond our human limitations to engage in a partnership that is otherworldly.

Relationship with God offers an opportunity for transcendence that is elusive like mist on a foggy morning but nevertheless utterly satisfying. It can't quite be captured or contained and will forever remain mysterious. Would we really want it any other way? Would we want God to be reducible to our level? Imagine the disregard we'd have for any love that would let us control the show. Would we want a dance partner that would only step where we allowed?

The profound truth about God is that we win! I don't mean we win over "those poor suckers," because certainly that is the antithesis of God. We win because we can't lose in God. There's no end and no beginning to love, and so in spending our life on this currency we only grow wealthier. Our bank account fills beyond what we can see and runs over into future generations.

Should we ever experience a shortage, we need only visit the vault for more than ample supply. Our buckets never run dry, and if we are found wanting bread, we are still satiated on Living Water. Any sense of lack is not because the Supply has withered but merely our intimate connection to it. We in fact hold the power of much of our fate. What kind of unconditional generosity is that? There is always room for more and we can have as much as we'd like!

Perception Challenge and Exercise

Human control hinders the ability to engage in relationship with the wonder and the mystery of God. It finds us rigid and unable to engage in the dance. Today, as you face challenges that come your way, rather than defaulting into anxiety, fear or panic, practice opening up to the vast Love of God that has been credited in full to your account. Envision releasing yourself into the expansive arms of an all-knowing Love that has already carried you across all divides. This is where the promise of the dance awaits you. You need merely acquiesce to the benevolence of God.

Uprising! New Belief: Letting go of the need for control opens up a whole new dimension that has no end and no beginning. Dancing with the mystery of God means you will never stop being surprised or in awe and wonder. There is no man-made or calculated substitute for faith. Choosing it over fear is an all-time leap and major uprising, over and over again. Practice it moment to moment for the greatest results. Faith allows you to engage in the dance with the mystery that is Love.

Repeat out loud: Instead of striving and pushing my way through life, today I will take a side road that allows me to gaze in wonder at what's before me. I will lift my eyes to notice the goodness and forbearance of God that has never stopped pursuing me. I will find amazement and peace in the depths of this outrageous Love and sufficiency for all of my needs. I choose faith over fear and abundance over scarcity. I choose the dance with mystery.

DAY 33: GOD PAINTS WITH A BROADER STROKE

As if putting on the emperor's new clothes, humankind falsely believes that by adding externally to ourselves we create significance. Yet it's said that the difficulty lies in the fact that we try to add substance to an unchanged consciousness.

The Internet Age unleashed an unprecedented war of hateful rants that expose the anger and confusion of many. There's a soberness in my spirit that silences my words and challenges my opinions. Jumping on the bandwagon and throwing my two cents in the pot would merely escalate the noise in this Tower of Babel. Remember the story of Babel? Because of their attempts to elevate their knowledge to Godlike proportions and replace their need for God, he caused every person to speak in a foreign language, leaving them unable to comprehend one another. I would say our ears are so dull from hearing that we find ourselves in a similar situation in which we desperately want to be heard but are only able to hear or understand ourselves.

What if there was no "right" side but merely humanity raging in the wind? What if there was something much bigger than right or wrong or what we can perceive with our natural sight?

God is eternally famous for holding the ultimate space of non-judgment towards humankind. Whether you believe it or not, get ahold of the picture. Although it's hard to wrap our heads around, he masterfully provided something far greater than our need to size up everything into right or wrong.

This is not to say that there are not real injustices in the world or that action should not take place. I am passionate about seeing the end of human trafficking and poverty. There is, however, a larger scope than I can imagine and history has been revealing it for some time.

As we've discussed, our insistent drive to point the finger, blame, judge and define what we perceive as right or wrong is the fruit of the Tree of the Knowledge of Good and Evil. The limitation in our perspective was superseded by God's abundant acceptance of humanity, but we've failed to recognize this provision.

While we want to study the facts and feed on information in the hopes of bringing transformation, God went behind the scenes on our behalf to level the playing field. That is what Love did and does every time we stand ready to accuse another or ourselves. I find this utterly mystical and too fabulous for words.

We often have much we think needs to be said, and sometimes it does. But fighting injustice in the same spirit of wrath and vengeance does not create change. Throwing stones at those who are no different than we are because we've failed to remove the plank in our own eyes or to see our own error or sin is the same as opposing the evil in others that we also possess.

What Spirit Are You Of?

Historically, true world changers have done things differently. They've not overtaken; they've served through love. Jesus is the ultimate example of serving through love, laying down his life, travailing for humanity and interceding on an entirely different plane. It's a particularly poignant love because the recipient rarely recognizes the need. There is plenty we can glean from this example of a vastly higher consciousness.

When our lens is zoomed in and we fail to see the entirety of the big picture—which by the way is *always*—we need to ask ourselves if we have the right to throw the stone. In case we're imagining that we do, let me clarify. From God's vantage point, he already took the hit by offering up his Son to cover our transgressions. He will forever stand to deflect and defend against accusation. He will defend us against our accusers as he will defend the ones we accuse. He made this exchange once and for all.

There is something far higher than accusation, determining a winner or loser or casting stones. Feeding from the dead mindset of the Tree of the Knowledge of Good and Evil can produce fruit only after its own kind: death, judgment and accusation. The Tree of Life produces life from Christ.

In a moment, I'll turn around and determine that I like one thing over another for lunch. I will constantly make judgments about what I choose and feast on things that fail to sustain me. I'll point my boney finger, cast judgment, keep score and live on the low level of determining good and evil, which is not my job. Without the guidance of the Spirit, I'll attempt to build a tower that is apart from God.

When we stand to accuse our brother, the Spirit is the one who convicts us and shows us the hardness of our heart if we're willing to humble ourselves to hear and receive. Before we take up our sword of words or actions, we need to understand what we are taking up and what spirit we are of. Are we in fact acting in the same spirit as those we oppose?

Perception Challenge and Exercise

Spirit helps us remember who we are and the nature that we carry. We carry our Father's nature, and Jesus is the exact representation of the Father and the first of many sons and daughters.

We see this illustrated here: "The Son radiates God's own glory and expresses the very character of God, and he sustains everything by the mighty power of his command" (Hebrews 1:3, NLT).

Challenge yourself to recognize the vast ground of God that resides within you and enables you to respect others, even though they may walk in hatred toward you. The Love of God propels us to love others in a way that is outside of ourselves.

Uprising! New Belief: Every day you have an opportunity to shift out of a "good and evil" vantage point and ascend into the kind of life and love that transcends circumstances and releases true freedom. The Spirit is your guide and is always revealing the mind of Christ within you. Embrace the ultimate life changer and mind bender!

Repeat out loud: I choose to see beyond the noise and fog of humanity into something greater. I choose this Life and other-worldly Love that I've been woven into. I say yes, I want to live beyond the argument. I want to be transformed by this Love that apprehends me and provides a supernatural grace and forbearance that is far too great to even comprehend. I say yes!

DAY 34: BREATHE IN THE ULTIMATE INTOXICATION

The seed form of everything is hidden until it is made manifest in the physical realm. Everything we're able to see was first made from an invisible, unseen realm. That's how creation works beneath the surface, in a very real but unseen atmosphere.

The Latin root of the word *creation* means "to bring forth." The world came into existence from the raw energy that already existed within God and was brought forth through full alignment and purpose. When the unlimited energy of God came forth, there was.

Similarly, until something is conceived in the mind and spoken out, "Let there be," those things that are invisible to the eye are delayed in coming forth into existence in our lives. This is why inner congruence and understanding our energy is so vital in determining what we are letting come forth.

Everything is made from spiritual energy and is waiting to respond to us. The spiritual realm is the causal realm where the seeds of our thoughts and beliefs are incubating. Imagine functioning at such a high energy and faith that the growth of the seeds rapidly accelerates in our life. The plump, faith-filled seeds burst forth into a quick manifestation as if traveling on a spiritual superhighway.

If ever there was a place to become a fast change artist, this is it. As we've seen, learning to redirect our thought life is essential to a happy life and is a key strategy in a life of faith. But a life or relationship with God is the superhighway where we ascend to the highest thoughts imaginable and unimaginable, thoughts beyond our to-do list and even our imagination of the possible. These thoughts provide alignment with divine purpose and direction. Intimate relationship with God is the highway.

Union

There is no formula or shortcut to bypass relationship. I might know your spouse, but I *know* my husband in a much deeper capacity because the two of us have become one. This is called "union."

My willingness to make my husband more important than all other men is what grows and strengthens our relationship. The intimacy of this relationship is better than all other distractions. Imagine how important that would be in our relationship with God, which surpasses human relationships.

When the Bible talks about "knowing" the love of Christ, it uses deeply relational language. For example, when Paul prays that the Ephesians may "know the love of Christ which surpasses knowledge" (Ephesians 3:19, NASB), the Greek word translated "know" is the same one used in other contexts to describe sexual intercourse.[19] Although it doesn't here imply literal intercourse, it does speak to how intense and intimate our relationship with God can be. Through the union of knowing Christ, we become one with him and can experience depth of relationship.

This suggests there exists through intimate union with Christ an exchange and intercourse that words cannot begin to describe. Loving intercourse between a husband and wife is a deeply spiritual experience that carries the individuals into a realm beyond themselves.

19   *Strong's Concordance*, s.v. "ginosko," #1097.

The very nature of union is beyond what we ourselves bring. We also take up another part. Although I give attention to my marriage, I don't "work to be better." I know that my husband loves me for who I am, not in the hope that I may become someone else. Imagine how ridiculous it would be if I was always working to be what I already am! It would be foolish to think union requires my effort when I'm already in it! The same is true with God, and that puts us smack-dab in the middle of completeness and union. We didn't make it happen.

The Gospel is the revelation that Christ died and we died with him! We are new creations; this is our true identity. Plenty of people struggle with this good news, even the ones who believe it. It's scandalous! It seems too good to be true! We can't seem to let go of the struggle and want to keep identifying with brokenness, but you and I are recipients of the mind and life of Christ. The old confused, anxious, depressed, sinful self went into the grave with Jesus.

We are told to be holy as Christ is holy and to be perfect as our Father in heaven is perfect. This is not a command but a provision. Through union with Christ, we're replaced and fully supplied. "I have been crucified with Christ and I no longer live, but Christ lives in me. The life I live in the body, I live by faith in the Son of God, who loved me and gave Himself for me" (Galatians 2:20, NIV). We think we need to do stupefying gymnastics to improve ourselves, but we simply need to enter into the grace that did away with the old us and made us new!

By all means, we need to check in with our feelings because they're informing us of the reality we believe, but remember there's something far greater than "good and evil." We've been pulled into divine life.

Faith isn't dictated by a feeling; it comes before a feeling. And faith has been supplied to us. We've been endowed with Love. We need only receive it!

"Because you have seen me, you have believed; blessed are those who have not seen and yet have believed" (John 20:29, NIV).

Perception Challenge and Exercise

Focusing on our limitations and weaknesses keeps us in a hole that we can't dig out of, but entraining to the higher energy of God's Love is the solution to all we need. This reality is the joy of relationship and the peace that comes with knowing you are a friend of God.

How might you transcend your current dilemmas or difficulties by believing in the greater reality of union where the "Let it be" of God was conceived and brought forth in you?

Stand in the River and experience the flow that does the work for you. Let the Spirit shift you out of negativity into life, truth and relationship. Be taken up into the heights far beyond your understanding or knowledge. Let go of all your "knowing" and enter into the realm of faith that carries you through your unknowing. You are fully loved and supported.

Uprising! New Belief: The biggest and best choice you can ever make is to recognize the reality of the Love relationship you're already wrapped up in. This recognition lifts you up above the scrounging and clawing to "make it happen" and enables you to enter into the ease of receiving love. Your actions are then a corresponding result of this belief and faith in

God's goodness, rather than a beggarly mentality of doubt, disbelief and fear. Become a fast change artist! Heck ya!

Repeat out loud: I was conceived through relationship, brought forth in relationship and cannot function apart from divine relationship, whether I recognize it or not. My heart chooses to stand in the beautiful invitation and mystery of this otherworldly relationship. I choose to flow and entrain to a higher way of being than I can even comprehend. I choose relationship with the Love of God and from there every possibility available. I am increasingly flowing in the River that supplies all life, nutrients and possibility. I am open and ready for Love!

DAY 35: UPRISING: WHAT YOU SEEK IS SEEKING YOU

Often people came to Jesus with questions but assumed they already had the answers. Jesus presented entirely new ways of thinking and seeing, posing different questions to upset and challenge the "knower's" perspective. He invited humanity's less-than-God vantage point to be expanded by God's exceeding wisdom.

"Truly, truly, I say to you, that the Son can do nothing of Himself, unless it's something He sees the Father doing" (John 5:19, NASB). Jesus taught that we would do well to set our minds on the Father's interest as well and not merely our own.

If Christ did nothing but what he saw the Father doing, what does that say to the rest of us? How often do we observe what the Father is initiating in our lives instead of running ahead and trying to direct the parade? If we're living from the Tree of the Knowledge of Good and Evil and valuing that which appears to be good, we'll easily miss what God's initiating. The appearance of good is an entirely different means of measuring and will never produce life.

Our focus determines our reality. As Jesus said, "I do nothing on my own initiative, but I speak these things as the Father taught me" (John 8:27, NASB). This totally flies in the face of our Western, make-it-happen-your-self mindset. The notion of flowing with the River, rather than forcing it, is foreign to us. How often have we initiated things that are lifeless because of our own self-interest?

The ability to discern what the Father is initiating comes through the Spirit. Although discernment can feel elusive, the more our gaze locks on our Father's eyes instead of others' good opinion, the more living in this manner becomes liberating.

Where are we going to go that exists outside of God? There is no place to hide and nowhere else to find life. We all came from God and are meant to find our life anchored in the Love of God.

Because Jesus was tied into what the Father was doing, he had an amazing perspective. Even though he would face crucifixion on the cross, he was able to say, "Oh death, where is your sting?" (1 Corinthians 15:55, NASB). When our eyes are locked with the Father's eyes, as Jesus' eyes were, we can remain undisturbed by life's challenges and able to say, "Death, where is your sting?"

Rumi said, "What you seek is seeking you." I think we often don't know what we're truly seeking. We think the current shiny object in view is what we're seeking. Yet, deep within, often beneath our conscious awareness, we long to know the Love that has been wooing us since before time began. We want to be loved like we've never been before, and God longs for nothing more than to love us the way he's always loved us. We all came from God, and so how could we not love God too, whether or not we recognize our Source yet?

We are wrapped up in the middle of this union that has brought us close, and we need only open our eyes to see. We are no longer flailing alone, needing to make it on our own, because God never ceases his intention to love us completely.

Perception Challenge and Exercise

As you end this week, carry with you God's underlying, overriding and intertwining purpose: "God so loved the world." You can't go anywhere to step outside of this intention.

You can't wake up in the morning with a burden that God doesn't plan to carry. You can't lie down at night overwrought with an anxiety that God does not wish to wipe away. You have always been loved with an everlasting Love, and there's nothing that will prevent this persuasion. What you seek, even if you don't know it, is seeking you! Believe it!

Uprising! New Belief: Some have said that humanity is like the ocean, a soup of turbulent and shifting waves. If this is true, the beauty about this is that Jesus not only calms the waves and reaches across them to find us in our loneliness and isolation, he dances across them to find us. We are invited up into the crescendo of this dance where love soothes our pain and satisfies our longing. We can simply let him love us.

Repeat out loud: Today I open my heart and life to the Love of God to be taken up into a romance of which I have barely scratched the surface. I will let Love pursue and apprehend me and never stop because this is not a human love, but an everlasting Love. I say yes! Love transform me!

WEEK 6:

Lover Is Your Identity

Day 36: Seeing the Invisible

Day 37: Words and Seeds

Day 38: We Are Lovers First

Day 39: Spiritual Insight

Day 40: Breathe In a Goodness and Promise Overload

Day 41: Laughing All the Way Home

Day 42: Uprising: You Are the Prize in God's Cracker Jack

INTRODUCTION TO WEEK 6

Lover Is Your Identity

Sometimes I think I don't quite know how to connect with God. I trip myself up through nasty comparisons of myself to others. This is evidence that I've temporarily forgotten that the Knower lives in me and is seeking himself in me!

Rohr tells us in *The Divine Dance*, "The Spirit is like a homing device put inside of you, and all creation, too. For all of our stupidity and mistakes, there's in everything this deep, internal dignity, convinced of its own value. This divine indwelling keeps insisting, 'I am what I am seeking!' This is surely what Jesus means when he says that all true prayers are already assured of their answer."[20]

And so we will spend this final week recognizing the One who is convinced of the value in us that he sees. How utterly surprised I imagine we would be to understand how heavily things have been rigged in our favor. Enjoy the discovery.

---

20   Rohr, *Divine Dance*, 151.

DAY 36: SEEING THE INVISIBLE

Prayer isn't about begging or deal making or trying to convince God that we will perform better so that our prayers will be answered. Rather, prayer is a connectedness—as Rohr reminds us, "It's God in you that loves God. It's God through you that recognizes God."[21]

As we stand in this flow as in a river, we are standing as the body of Christ with authority and prayer moving through us. It is when our desires are God-directed and our heart says, "Let it be done unto me as you have said," that we are in true alignment and agreement.

"Let it be done unto me as you have said" were Mary's words. "Mary, who is the personification of the human race receiving the Christ, shows us that our 'let it be' matters to God—God does not come into our worlds un-invited. Spirit needs a Mary, a body, a womb, a humanity that says, 'I want you'—your yes is always God's yes."[22]

Prayer is an opening and aligning where we enter into the invitation for relationship and merge with God's will; it's not a performance or song and dance posture. It's stepping into the place of communion and indwelling Presence where we perceive what God is doing and join in. This is not to presumptuously believe that God thinks the way we do and agrees with our opinions, but rather that the Christ life within us calibrates at a higher level and we are invited to enter into it.

21   Rohr, *Divine Dance*, 151.
22   Rohr, *Divine Dance*, 153.

The Downfall of Natural-Mindedness

How often are we stuck in the cul-de-sac of human thought and reasoning that keeps us circling the limitations of our perspective and excluded from the life supply within us? This very perspective is why we are exhorted, "Do not judge according to appearance" (John 7:24, NASB).

The very limited confines of the law of human perspective and natural sight blind us to and bind us to the realm of appearance, for the law keeps us relegated to limitation because it will never produce life. However, we are exhorted, "If you are led by the Spirit, you are not under the law" (Galatians 5:18, NASB).

As long as we wallow in the low realm of law, information, seeking others' opinions and focusing on what we can see or understand, we are propagating what is destined to fade away. However, "Faith is the substance of things hoped for, the evidence of things not seen" (Hebrews 11:1, KJV). Through faith we are enabled to look further into the unseen realm and believe in what's possible. It's the Spirit that breathes faith into our hearts and awakens us out of the slumber of our shortsighted vision and mindsets.

Walter Lanyon eloquently describes this for us:

> I was a child with a small measure at the seaside, trying to
> carry off a little water when the whole sea was at my disposal,
> and I understood for the first time the exhaustless sea of
> substance about me, and the idea of hoarding was but a
> childish fear grown into a Goliath by false teaching and
> beliefs. I suddenly became aware that the substance was every-

where, in everything, out of everything, and the only place of lack was in the hypnotic state of belief—and I alone created and moved in this vacuum.[23]

It is effortless to move out of the limitation of rationale into the instant expansion and openness to "Let there be" by simple acknowledgement, produced not through will or strife but agreement. Faith is as simple as agreeing with God, who has from the beginning breathed life out of nothing and made it appear.

Life Pictured

"Truly, truly, I say to you, whoever hears my word and believes him who sent me has eternal life. He does not come into judgment, but has passed from death to life" (John 5:24, ESV).

This passing from death to life is the Christ life told and retold throughout the Old and New Testaments of the Bible from one picture to the next. The Old Testament tells of the food from heaven that was given to our fathers in the wilderness long ago, called manna, but we have been given a superior food they didn't know about. We are blessed through recognizing this Presence and provision given to us.

This is what the manifestation of "before we call, we are answered" looks like, because we believe that what we ask already exists in spite of opposing evidence to the contrary. To see the manifestation, it must first be recognized in the invisible realm, and as we discussed above, "Faith is the substance of things hoped for, the evidence of things not seen." What we ask for already exists and is ready to manifest.

Until we are willing to believe that life springs from the invisible, we separate ourselves in our minds from the propagating influence of life. When we strive to bring forth from outside of our being, we invariably continue to experience barrenness through a divided consciousness, but "by faith we understand that the worlds were prepared by the word of God, so that what is seen was not made out of things which are visible" (Hebrews 11:3, NASB). This is a deep well that we could drink from forever!

The clincher is that seeing is not what produces believing, but faith to believe in the unseen, which opens our blind eyes and closed ears. That's why we're told to "strengthen the feeble hands, steady the knees that give way; say to those with fearful hearts, 'Be strong, do not fear...' Then will the eyes of the blind be opened and the ears of the deaf unstopped. Then will the lame leap like a deer, and the mute tongue shout for joy. Water will gush forth in the wilderness and streams in the desert" (Isaiah 35:3–6, NIV).

Mind Shifts

The mind that dwells in anxiety blocks the ever-flowing substance of the River and remains in famine, but the consciousness that gives itself to the Infinite discovers torrents of substance and provision, flowing freely, being given even before we ask.

"But everything exposed by the light becomes visible—and everything that is illuminated becomes a light. This is why it is said: 'Awake, O sleeper, rise up from the dead, and Christ will give you light' " (Ephesians 5:14,

ESV). This Christ light is what illuminates our sight to see beyond a barren desert into a gushing oasis, to see beyond drought into ultimate provision and to see Presence everywhere.

The experience of drought in our lives shows that we are still judging from the appearance of things. As we begin to look to Spirit and believe that the Christ life within us is our ample supply, we will encounter the Source of satisfaction and all provision. It is said, "I will open rivers on the bare heights and springs in the midst of the valleys; I will make the wilderness a pool of water and the dry land fountains of water" (Isaiah 41:18, NASB). One of the definitions for the word translated "fountains" in this verse is "going forth." I have heard it said that this fountain and source of satisfaction is what allows us to continually go forth.[24]

When we feel our river has become a dried-up water hole, we need only look again at the essence of River, the unconditional Love, grace and favor that washes away every sense of lack, and there we'll discover the true Source of satisfaction. This is where we exercise our faith muscle to see the invisible, knowing the Love of God is completely untarnished and ample. Where there is fear, we have not seen love rightly, because there is no fear in love. Fear carries with it a sense of dread and punishment (1 John 4:8, NIV).

Abundance is a lens that says, "There's no separation between Love and me." It says, "I was always wrapped up in love and always will be." Divine Love is the ultimate Source and abundance. It is restorative and healing. When we rightly direct our focus, we will access the unlimited abundance of God that awakens our spirit to the Source of all life and provision.

---

24   *Strong's Concordance*, s.v. "motsa," #4161.

Lanyon reminds us that we are not encouraged to revere the riches of Solomon's robe, but rather to notice the ways of the lily. The lily suddenly appears out of the unseen. "No one thinks it strange when he plants a lily-bulb that a lily should appear in due season. Why should it be strange then, that prayer is actually answered?"[25] Prayer is recognition of who God is and not begging for what we fear he is not.

And so we are encouraged not to look at appearances, but to cast the weight of our cares on the shoulders of the One whose ways are higher than ours. As we look to the Source of Life, we are clothed in the radiance of Life.

Perception Challenge and Exercise

How often, as you look out into the barren ground surrounding you, do you set your gaze on what is lacking instead of setting it on what is about to arise? There is no way to see beyond the difficulties you often face in life without a spiritual perspective and encounter.

You are challenged daily to see beyond what is right in front of your eyes and to direct your heart and mind in the way you would have them go. Seeing the invisible takes faith, and faith has been granted to you for the apprehending. Practice setting your gaze on the unchanging goodness of God, even though the human heart has not even imagined the depths of this expansive Love. Determine to believe and continue discovering!

Uprising! New Belief: We've talked time and time again about the notion that happiness is within reach when we determine that our reality is not based upon what we can hold within our fingers, but what we believe with our heart. We have been given all things needed to live an empowered life. Isn't it time that we embrace the all and determine never to settle for less?

Repeat out loud: I believe that I am loved and will walk in the abundance of this unconditional Love. I will set my gaze on the unseen realm and discover the miraculous Oasis in the surrounding deserts of life. I will apprehend the faith that has been bestowed on me through the Love of God so that very soon I will not even see a desert.

DAY 37: **WORDS AND SEEDS**

I bet if we recall the greatest things that have come into our life, they have been gifts that we've had little to do with: friendships, children, spouses and daily surprises. Aside from showing up and breathing, I had nothing to do with the family I was born into, the husbands I was miraculously gifted, the children I conceived or the many wonders that have graced my life.

Certainly we work hard, and our efforts produce paychecks, grown children, strengthened relationships and health, yet God is able to produce far beyond all that is within our scope of knowing and manifesting. Our need to know is the cord that tethers us to all that becomes a barrier to faith and receiving.

In this moment, if we were given the gift that we so desperately crave, would we be able to receive it? When we hold onto the "law" of our rationale, we're doomed with explanations and reasons why things can't be so. And we find that "there is a way that seems right, but in the end leads to death" (Proverbs 14:12, NIV).

We often continue the cycle of believing strongly in lack, and so we continue to reproduce it while our need or desire escapes our grasp. We may muster a few affirmations while disbelieving what we spout. Nevertheless, the truth is that the desert abounds with seed and plentiful blossoms.

Lanyon tells us that as we stop judging from appearances, we are "breaking the enchantment" of human thought in and surrounding us.[26] How-

---

26   Lanyon, *Laughter of God*, 56–57.

ever, rather than following this exhortation, we often set our focus on the problem we want to rectify and try to attack and destroy what we perceive as evil, so the very thing we desire to destroy destroys us.

Awakening to Christ-consciousness means no longer looking at the surrounding appearances and off into the future for good to come, but living from the now reality of being "absent in the body, but present in Spirit" (1 Corinthians 5:3, NASB). Christ-consciousness means our focus is on an otherworldly reality that will never be shaken or destroyed, despite circumstances.

Thirsty?

Isaiah prophesied, "Come, all who are thirsty, come to the waters; and you who have no money, come, buy and eat!...As the rain and the snow come down from heaven, and do not return to it without watering the earth and making it bud and flourish, so that it yields seed for the sower and bread for the eater, so is my word that goes out from my mouth: It will not return to me empty, but will accomplish what I desire and achieve the purpose for which I sent it" (Isaiah 55:1, 8–11, NIV).

Imagine faith that receives these words as seeds bursting forth into reality and provision, despite what can be seen on the horizon. Imagine freely eating that which sustains and produces life.

In the same manner, Peter, Jesus' disciple, told a lame beggar, "Silver and gold I do not have, but what I do have I give to you" (Acts 3:6, NIV). The beggar received the gift and was instantly healed and able to walk.

What if, as pictured in this story, we were able to recognize our lowly and beggarly thoughts and through faith receive Life within? It is the Father's good pleasure to give us Life, enabling us to be free of every kind of limitation. What if we're able to recognize the gift that is more precious than gold or silver and, like the lame beggar, go on our way rejoicing?

Does this mean that every person is healed, hospitals are emptied and the world turns into Candy Land? I believe it's possible to see abundant supernatural healings. I have lost loved ones to illness and suffered illness within my own body, but instead of turning the blame onto the One that is perfect Love, I think how grave a mistake and diversion it is to spend my days and my thoughts on less than what is available to me. I don't want to waste a minute on anything other than the ultimate Captivation, and yet sadly I often do.

Again we are reminded that it's not so much what *is* that hinders us. It's what we tell ourselves about what we think is so, but isn't! Paul reminds us not to walk in the futility of our mind, being darkened in our understanding, which excludes us from the life of God because of our own ignorance and hardness of heart (Ephesians 4:17–8, NASB).

Isaiah tells us not to point our finger or speak words of wickedness, but instead to give ourselves to the hungry and satisfy the afflicted. Then our light will break forth, our gloom will become like the brightness of midday and we will be like a well-watered garden (Isaiah 58:7–11, NASB). Interestingly, we might think this is great advice to receive concerning the treatment of others, but did you know that the word for *afflicted* here actually carries the definitions "depress, abase self, browbeat, chasten self, deal hardly, submit self, afflict, mishandle and put down," just to name a few?[27]

27   *Strong's Concordance*, s.v. "anah," #6031a.

If we eliminate the pointing of our finger and speaking wickedly of ourselves, imagine the light that will burst forth within and around us that will lead us out of the "futility of our mind" into the overflowing life intended for us.

We get to choose to remain living below our capacity or believe this admonition. I choose to feed myself with that which is life and makes my faith come alive, rather than stay in the muck of negativity, fear and scarcity. What about you?

Perception Challenge and Exercise

If you're like me, you wake up many a morning thirsty for peace, calm and sight that are far beyond your own. Thankfully, there's a soothing drink to satisfy the thirst. There's a wonderful River that is free for the taking where you can have your fill and more.

Look around and you will notice that many stay parched. Trying to subdue your own affliction and ill self-treatment with substitutes will never have the capacity to satisfy you; all the while, the Word of life is within reach.

Life is consistently challenging, but you have a choice to seek the substance of Presence over counterfeits and quality over quantity. Will you always choose correctly? Sadly, the answer is often no. Nevertheless, you will never be turned away from the pure drink of God's Love when you awaken to the River within. You won't be truly content unless you stay hooked up to the water supply. Want to be drinking buddies?

Uprising! New Belief: It might take a little while to wrap your mind around this idea and open your spirit to the reality that there is nothing closer than the Presence of God that dwells within. But once you do, you will find an amazing exchange of quiet for noise, calm for angst and peace for your self-inflicted inner violence. It's only an acknowledgement and recognition away.

Clearly, you know that peace is not found in the fun new diversion, new outfit, perfect job, long-awaited lover or bank account—it's within you. When you're willing to step away from the hustle and bustle of entice-ments, you will find the best enticement imaginable. When you're willing to be present and let go of excuses and space-filling lovers, you will awak-en to true satisfaction. You wouldn't be reading this if you weren't ready and hadn't been making the shift all along this journey. Welcome to the ultimate upgrade.

Repeat out loud: I have entangled myself with many a diversion. I have danced with many a lover and none have satisfied me the way I long to be satisfied. None have poured down on my thirstiness and quenched my in-ner drought. There is no one else that can water the soil within me where God has planted himself, the place where God calls me to him and to my-self. And so I say yes, and I will say it anew every morning. Yes, I choose the Lover that has never stopped loving me, nor ever will, to be my unending intoxication and life to my soul.

DAY 38: WE ARE LOVERS FIRST

Jesus said that it's the truth that sets us free, and Byron Katie reminds us that arguing with it is why we're miserable.[28] It's the illusion that we constantly drag into the argument that trips us up. Sadly, we'd often rather validate the appearance of things around us than believe the truth.

I refuse to let indifference, withholding of love and affirmation from others, judgment, law-keeping or my own unmet expectations be the criteria for invalidating myself in an inner debate.

Paul tells us, "I implore you to examine faith for yourselves in order to test what it is that you really believe. Faith is so much more than the mere veneer of a superstitious belief in historic Christ; faith is about realizing Jesus Christ in you, in the midst of contradiction! Just like when ore is placed into a crucible, and when the dross is separated from the gold in a furnace; come to the conclusion for yourselves of his indwelling! Should it appear to you that Christ is absent in your life, look again, you have obviously done the test wrong!" (2 Corinthians 13:5, *Mirror Bible*).

Francois Du Toit breaks down what Paul is relaying to us in this way: "There is only one valid faith, not what we believe about God or about ourselves, but what God believes about us! God is persuaded about Christ indwelling you, now he wants you to be equally persuaded!" Du Toit goes on to say, "Self examination has nothing to do with finding hidden sins and flaws in you; it is all about realizing Christ in you! The object of the furnace is not to reveal the dross, but the gold!"[29] The only way to see the gold in

---

28   Byron Katie, *Loving What Is* (New York: Three Rivers Press, 2002), 119.

others or us is through the eyes of Love. And it is Love that was in us from the beginning.

It is often through a greater recognition of God's love towards us that we encounter Love reflected in us, as André Rabe describes in *Desire Found Me*:

> Man's first and formative conscious experience, according to this Genesis account, is of God's adoration, God's blessing, God's self-giving love. To absorb and reflect this love is to participate in this relationship of likeness. Humanity is all God imagines her to be as she beholds the One who adores her, allowing this adoration to define her as she reflects it back. "We love, because He first loved us" (1 John 4:19, NASB). This is a vision of ideal reflection, ideal mimesis. God's desire for me awakens my desire for him. His relentless pursuit of me sustains my passion for him. I have found my true reflection. In this place of mutual exchange there is no rivalry. This "likeness" does not create the desire to replace the other but to partake of the other. Intimacy rather than rivalry is the result. Even God's otherness does not frighten me but entices me to explore.[30]

Lovers

Love made its mark in us long ago, and because of it we are lovers. Lovers are who we are, and this identity will never change. Naturally, every time we put something before this reality, we're going to get tripped up by a transitory title, occupation and identity that keeps us living far below our true identity. Nevertheless, it does not alter who God says that we are.

To live separate from this identity negates the powerful life within us and

---

29   Francois Du Toit, *The Mirror Bible*, commentary on 2 Corinthians 13:5 (Hermanus, South Africa: Mirrorword Publishing, 2012), 160.

30   André Rabe, *Desire Found Me* (Andre Rabe Publishing, 2014), 42.

hinders the fuel to our flame. Brennan Manning describes the fire of Love like this:

> The gospel is absurd and the life of Jesus is meaningless unless we believe that he lived, died, and rose again with but one purpose in mind: to make brand-new creations. Not to make people with better morals but...men and women who would surrender to the mystery of the fire of the Spirit that burns within, who would live in ever greater fidelity to the omnipresent Word of God, who would enter into the center of it all, the very heart and mystery of Christ, into the center of the flame that consumes, purifies, and sets everything aglow with peace, joy, boldness, and extravagant, furious love.[31]

Lovers live on a different plane. They don't view or speak to one another in a judgmental, condemning tone, because they're living from love and not the eye of judgment. Those that fail to see the love and beauty others carry fail to see or experience it within themselves, because they know God only as a rule keeper instead of as an intimate lover. When we identify a nagging corrective message or tone in our head, we're identifying our view of God, believing that we have failed to deserve love. The truth is, Love has already decided on us! We simply have to believe it!

Undeniable Intoxication

Lovers live with an undeniable intoxication that even flows out onto those around them. They radiate intoxication because they have been close to the fire and because they are imbibing the potent elixir, Love.

---

31   Brennan Manning, *The Furious Longing of God* (Colorado Springs, CO: David C. Cook, 2009), 124–26.

The word *imbibe* means:

1. to consume...

2. to absorb or soak up, as water, light or heat: *Plants imbibe moisture from the soil.*

3. To take or receive into the mind, as knowledge, ideas, or the like: *to imbibe a sermon; to imbibe beautiful scenery...*

4. To soak or saturate; imbue.[32]

Puritanical folks have struggled with the fact that Jesus enjoyed imbibing wine. For goodness sake, he even turned water into wine—and not just any wine, but the best the guests had tasted all day (John 2:10, NASB). What is the message?

I imagine he was pointing out the fact that there is lasting wine that no other intoxication can rival. He reserves that wine for the guests that stick around and who are close friends and family. To those he offers a depth of full-bodied richness that deeply satisfies.

You can show up but leave early and fill up on dribble, or you can be counted as a friend and lover that will be satiated and intoxicated on unending Love! There's simply no substance that will leave a lasting effect like imbibing the Love of God. It's transformational.

Perception Challenge and Exercise

32   Dictionary.com, s.v. "imbibe."

Love is the one thing that draws us all and has us searching the ends of the earth. What if you've had it all along? What if the desire for Love has been Love pursuing you from the very beginning?

Whether you recognize it or not, that fire and heartbeat of God already beats for you, in your heart. It's not about your belief system, a list of do's and don'ts, but a passion that's always burned for you. How does it feel to be forever wanted and pursued?

Uprising! New Belief: It might seem too wild to fathom, but intoxicated is how we are meant to live, not through abusing substances but through drinking the pure presence of God. You were made for Love and by Love, so why would Love's intoxication be simply expressed in select moments, like in our Sunday best? Why would you settle for intellectual knowledge about God when you could dine with him?

You can choose the mere veneer of propriety and miss out on the depths of Love, but how unsatisfying is that when your heart beats for the scandalous Love of God that is too extravagant to be contained? What a grand and intoxicating venture. Spend your days pondering the fervent and intoxicating goodness of the Love of God. I dare ya!

Repeat out loud: I am a lover and was made for Love, not tepid but intoxicating romance with God. I embrace the gold that was identified in me before I was even born. I am called beloved and that will never change. I am the apple of God's eye and refuse to see myself in any other manner. I am a lover!

DAY 39: **SPIRITUAL INSIGHT**

Let's be honest: we want all the bling without the darkness that makes the light shine so brightly. We want clarity, vision and answers without any sense of doubt. We want life without death and total control over things that allow us to get our way, never realizing that we have *God with us*, the indwelling life that carries us through our darkness into resurrection and rebirth time and time again. Every morning we are born again to welcome each new day as our lungs are filled with breath, life and Spirit!

The Spirit guide we're given enables us to access creative power, not occasionally or at one time in history as if God were static, but always and continuously. This guide is not some far-off and out-of-reach deity, but part of the Love flow of God impacting the ever-expanding universe. And to confirm this, the scientific community tells us that we are still discovering new planets and stars that have never been identified before. There is definitely nothing stagnant here!

The beautiful mystery of God takes us out of the vertical, misguided, hierarchical pyramid of a Zeus-like God throwing lightning bolts and needing appeasement and moves us into a horizontal—or better yet, circular—and open-ended interface through relationship. The spiral never ends. As in all healthy relationships, discovery of each other continues and remains in the present tense.

Relationship spirals in a back-and-forth context of giving and receiving. The unity and flow between the Father and Son, the Son being the exact representation of the Father, is breathtaking (Hebrews 1:3, NIV). The dance and flow of Spirit that draws us up into this family circle surpasses the cleverest choreography.

Spirit moves in perfect union within relationship in the will of God and as God, being the ultimate creative expression in perfect conjunction with God's highest thought and innovative wisdom. There is no rival for position, but utter give and take, preference and submission one to another, not practiced or rote, but alive and breathed in the moment.

When we recognize that this mystical relationship is the life in us that we're brought into and that there's no top to arrive at, no human-centered appeasing to strive toward, we can rest in the Presence and ease of receiving. We are counted as part of the unchanging and indwelling Love of God: "The Spirit of God has made me and the breath of the Almighty gives me life" (Job 33:4, NIV).

Seeing Differently

Although we began the discussion on Day 36 at the beginning of the week, there is more to explore around seeing into the invisible realm and the expansion of senses that some religions represent as the third eye. Rightly so: it's beyond human sight. This kind of sacred seeing comes through the eye of the heart.

The eye is the light or lamp of the body. When the eye is single (that is, clear and focused), the whole body is full of light (Luke 11:34, KJV). This extension of consciousness is what Jesus was referring to when he said to "look again," to see and perceive differently (2 Corinthians 10:7, NASB).

The recognition of Presence and Oneness of eternal Heaven within us is what allows us to see beyond the appearance of what Lanyon describes as "a thousand and one beliefs armed to the teeth and out-pictured as an army of horsemen and chariots. Debts, impossible situations, disease, fears—all of these things have come and blocked the only way."[33]

There are hundreds of stories that remind us that the recognition of Presence is the "looking again" that relays and initiates the extension of vision and singleness of sight.

Even the Son of God recognized that although he could do all things, he could do nothing of himself. He was intertwined through the Relationship that expands vision. Relying on natural senses and abilities—which judge only by appearance—is what keeps us in limitation, trapped by the "army of horsemen" in a duality of "good and evil."

The Presence of Spirit leads us to see on an entirely different plane of life. Recognizing the Kingdom of Heaven within suddenly elevates us into a new dimension of single focus, where we see things that have already been prepared, rather than things we're struggling to make happen.

It is written, "No eye has seen, no ear has heard, and no mind has imagined what God has prepared for those who love him" (1 Corinthians 2:9, NLT). For most of us, steeped as we are in a world that focuses on appearance and willpower to make things happen, it's mind-bending to suddenly comprehend the ease of receiving the "already prepared" waiting for us beyond our natural senses!

---

33   Walter Lanyon, *The Temple Not Made With Hands*
      (Glen Ellyn, IL: Union Life Ministries, 1977), 33.

This invitation is open to all and is outside of any man-made system. It's offered to anyone who will toss off the shrouds of human thinking and recognize the Presence of God.

Taste and See

The generosity of divine Love that allows for this expansion is mind-blowing. What does that say about the value of the recipients? This Oneness that is granted to us, this intertwining spiritual identity, is sight to our blindness, long-range spectacles for our human shortsightedness and hearing to our deafness.

This generosity is what "Taste and see that the Lord is good" (Psalm 34:8, NIV) is all about, and yet how is it possible to taste God? There's certainly mystery wrapped up in God, as well as the need to look further for insight, such as gleaning that "man shall not live by bread alone, but every word which proceeds out of the mouth of God" (Matthew 4:4, NASB).

As I mentioned at the beginning of the week, our forefathers were provided manna in the wilderness and yet died, but we have been given Bread that they didn't know in the person of Jesus, whose descent from heaven brings unending life (John 6:49–51, NIV). This supernatural sustenance is articulated further in Jesus' saying, "If you knew the gift of God and who it is that asks you for a drink, you would have asked him and he would have given you living water...Whoever drinks the water I give them will never thirst" (John 4:10, 14, NIV).

This tasting is more profound than a mere sip and far greater than a deep well of problems. Yet all these pictures take us beyond appearance into where Jesus filled the gap of empty plates to overflowing abundance, which is illustrated through "taste and see," "look again" and "you have manna you know not of."

Supposing that there was such sustenance, what good would it be if we couldn't taste it? Historical facts, the letter of the law and perfect performance all leave us empty. Information does nothing without Spirit enabling an expansion of our human senses. So when we truly "taste," we find the confines of our natural understanding expand and suddenly we receive all manner of the wine of Life and its overflowing intoxication that leaves information and the "letter of the law" on their knees.

However, only those who taste, rather than pontificate about the legalities of right and wrong, are the ones to receive the joy of this living Bread. These are the ones who refuse to settle for religious hoopla and instead sup on the everlasting intoxication and life of "If anyone hears my voice and opens the door, I will come into him and dine with him, and he with me" (Revelations 3:20, NASB).

The contagiousness of one who has tasted and seen the goodness and outrageous benevolence of God displays radiance that cannot be hidden. It's like a city on a hill or a gleaming diamond in the most beautiful setting. And most wonderfully, Presence ushers in freedom, which is the signature of divine Love and acceptance.

God is Love, not a control freak. You cannot find a myopic, stingy or withholding rule keeper that has been awakened to the Love of God. The two are polar opposites because the vantage point of Love is just too vast. Knowing this should help us have love and compassion for those judgers that have yet to truly "taste and see" the goodness of God.

Oh, that our natural senses would be expanded into the spiritual dimension! We would experience a million-star canopy that pulls us up out of our illusions of struggle, withholding and forgottenness and plops us right back into "look again" where we "taste and see" unending Love. The presence of Spirit is the ever-pulsating light that catapults through our darkened unknowing and offers us night vision.

Perception Challenge and Exercise

Imagine the frequency and sight of the sweet melodies of faith that make every moment a happy hour! Oh, how the atmosphere around you and in your life will be impacted as you open your eyes to truly see. Explore the invitation to open the door and "taste and see" the goodness awaiting you! You might even try on the sweetness that I hear when I am addressed as "Baby Girl" by the Lover of my soul.

Uprising! New Belief: Just because you haven't known that other planets or stars existed doesn't mean that they haven't been quietly awaiting your awareness. The wide-open invitation to the Presence of God needs but an acknowledgement; "look again," and recognition is on its way. The Kingdom of Heaven is at home in you, and all you need do is recognize it! Open your eyes and awaken to the prepared-before-time-began-goodness and drink it in.

Repeat out loud: I have been brought into the most glorious mystical union and relationship with God. I set my gaze to the ever-expanding single vision where I am able to access the depths of love and find that I am seated right in the middle of all the "prepared for me" goodness!

DAY 40: BREATHE IN A GOODNESS AND PROMISE OVERLOAD

The seven years I was a single mother of four seemed like an eternity of men running for their lives. Yet I had regular encouragement stirring within me that I would remarry. Every time discouragement nagged at my heels, I soon discovered new and often ridiculous promises of the "already prepared" that seemed an impossible notion of marrying off a mom with four young children.

I've heard it said, "Any time there is a delay, it's because an increase is coming." An increase is interpreted as an upgrade. Instead of settling for "this will do," a delay has a promise lingering in the coffers that exceeds expectation if we have faith to believe it.

Certainly, during the delay, that notion lands as utter ridiculousness upon our desperation, highlighting in neon lights our barren desert. And then, what's this, the strange and mystical rainbow hanging as a promise in the sky? It's even painted in childlike colors that seem unreal to our adult thinking. And we're supposed to believe and hold out for the goodness of the promise? God loves to confound our human wisdom in childlike displays!

We want the promise with the lightning speed with which we get a hamburger from our favorite drive-thru restaurant. We want it now, and when now is delayed we immediately decide it isn't coming.

I never recall one of my children receiving a long-awaited surprise and refusing to believe its legitimacy. I recall plenty of whining during the waiting, but like childbirth, the pain quickly turns to joy with the arrival of the gift. That's why we are encouraged to rehearse and remember the promises of God's great works and to dwell upon all the great things he has done (Psalm 143:5, NLT).

The Promise

I have entered a new season where all the longing for unrequited friendship, partnerships and opportunities that before hung just out of reach suddenly seems hilarious to me. I find myself blessing the absent ones that aren't in my life and experiencing an uncommon joy over the prospect of the right things, rather than the craved-for things. I'm simply giddy about opportunity, provision and relationships that are meant to be in my life that appear at the right time. I am elated that I have not received what I thought I wanted, because what I thought I wanted was far inferior to all that has been prepared for me.

I haven't always been in this place, and I may again find myself in the state where I've thrown fits, cried, longed and fought with God for what felt withheld. But now I am giddy with delight. Why would I claw my way in an attempt to get anything less than the best? Think about it. That's insanity!

Timing Is Everything

Honestly, when we're waiting for the delivery we could care less about correct timing, believing this is as darn good a time as any! But truth be told, if I had not waited seven lonely, difficult years for my husband Mark, I probably wouldn't have recognized the gift that he is. Being a girl that likes bling, I would have overlooked his unassuming and gentle nature. If I hadn't rented for six years, would I have been grateful for our sweet little

'60s fixer-upper that quickly turned into our haven of rest? I doubt it!

We need to accept that we truly don't want anything before its time. When a baby arrives prematurely, it brings severe complications that threaten its survival. We don't want anything prematurely. We want all of the wonderful things God has prepared for us, but not before we're ready to handle or receive them.

During seasons of waiting and transitioning into the new, we are reminded not to judge from appearances, but to recognize the Oneness of life. This shift in perception changes our whole posture. Remember, when our eye is single, the whole body is full of light (Luke 11:34, KJV). There is no better recognition than knowing *no one* has taught us the things we've learned; they have come straight from the indwelling life of God.

During the wait, we should turn our focus to:

- Rehearse the goodness of God and recall his faithfulness in our lives that has gotten us to this point.

- Recognize how God's Presence fills up all sense of lack in our life.

- Learn to see the unseen germinating below the surface as the right climate causes promises to spring up.

- Celebrate the gifts that are amply surrounding us presently.

- Recognize and appreciate with joyful expectation the more around us, and more will begin to expand before our eyes.

- Joyfully cultivate gratitude for the breath we are given to breathe today.

One day, when we have moved on to new circumstances and surroundings, we will realize that these were the good old days, so let's not waste this time looking off into the future in want of something else. Let's live today to the fullest, believing we have everything we need and recognizing that the things we think we need we're simply not ready for—they're still germinating below the surface. Good things are coming. Believe it!

Perception Challenge and Exercise

It's entirely human to want things to happen quickly and in your own timetable, but it reveals a lot about your faith level and need for refueling when setbacks and delays derail you. The failure of a promise to appear in your time frame implies nothing about the probability of its happening in the future. The challenge is to keep your heart encouraged and hope-filled as you continue to recount all the good that surrounds you. Cultivate keeping yourself in faith!

Uprising! New Belief: Those who practice the Presence of God recognize that Spirit is the oil that keeps the lamp burning. It is the fuel that lights and warms the heart, infusing hope when there is no evidence on the horizon. Although you'll have seasons when you struggle to hold onto faith and hope, choosing to believe in God's goodness is the act of faith that continues to look to the future with positive anticipation. It is the choice that continues to lift you up and refocus your sight so that you can behold the promise incubating on your behalf. It takes courage to refuse to believe any other alternative than the perfect Love of God. Congratulations on your bravery!

Repeat out loud: In life, even though delays are inevitable, I choose to believe that God has it covered. Nothing prepared for me from the abundance of God's goodness and kindness can be withheld from me. God is working behind the scenes on my behalf and setting the stage for all things concerning me. I will keep my face pointed toward the sunshine where I won't see or focus on the shadows.

DAY 41: LAUGHING ALL THE WAY HOME

When I was in high school, I remember the students returning from a several-months-long Outward Bound experience. Their faces seemed different because they *were* different. The veneer of the old high school posture was gone. Ego's aloof and proud saunter stayed behind in the woods, and in its place was pure joy and ease of self-knowing and tranquility. Maybe that is why it's said, "Happiness can always be recollected in tranquility."[34]

It's hard work carrying an image of something other than ourself, and it's hard work trying to bury the person we're afraid to reveal for fear of scorn or never truly feeling embraced. All of that grief and self-rejection has to go somewhere. No wonder many of us have zapped energy and poor health! I have certainly struggled with these issues in my life. I write what I live because there is no power in our words if they do not come from truth.

Lanyon writes, "Anything, when not recognized, dies—and the old inflated ego needed the winds of acclaim and praise to keep the balloon afloat." [35] Imagine the freedom and joy of releasing the garb of ego and letting it go and finding within oneself the truth that ushers in the most welcoming safe haven. People seldom know that instead of accepting the truth within themselves, they have merely learned survival techniques that curtail the opportunity for discovering it. That is why I am such a proponent of the discovery that takes place through life coaching.

We all need self-permission to find our way home. It's a sort of coming-of-age reality that is appropriate at any age. I find that even outspoken people who believe they're living with confidence and security are often

---

34   Spoken by Lord Melbourne in the series *Victoria* by Daisy Goodwin. (*Victoria*, "Brocket Hall," series 1, episode 3, directed by Tom Vaughan, written by Daisy Goodwin, ITV, aired September 4, 2016.)

35   Lanyon, *The Temple Not Made With Hands*, 11.

cloaking their secret frailty behind a mask. So for all of us, the things we've discussed up to this point are treks on the journey, like a roadmap home. Oh what joy to finally be able to come home!

The Joy Road

There is no faster road to joy and happiness than becoming a welcoming abode for oneself. Learning to laugh at ourself is a million-dollar antidote! Even as I typed the sentence below in my usual manner of writing, words popping into my head and then looking them up to see if they're real or imagined Kimberisms, I broke into laughter! At times I amuse myself to no end. However, I am certain that if I did it much more often, I would be that much more entertained!

Although I write, I certainly have never pretended to be an English teacher or grammatical wizard, and so before landing on the word *drudgery* below, I typed in *trudgery*! Thank goodness for editors! Some grammar police are astounded at those of us that bare our weaknesses on social media for the world to see.

Once a woman responded to my tweet, saying that I was an idiot and as a self-proclaimed wordsmith she could help me! She certainly made me laugh, right before I blocked her! Really, insult me and then offer your services? I laugh just thinking about it.

I am thrilled that I give myself permission to write, as with so many things, without perfection! It's when we determine that we've gotten it perfect that we should heed the words attributed to Mark Twain: "It's not what you don't know that kills you, it's what you think you know for sure that ain't so."

WEEK 6

Outrageous Joy

Life can be difficult, but it was never meant to be joyless drudgery or trudgery! What if we're called into account one day for the platter full of life and experiences before us that we failed to celebrate and enjoy? What a thought! That's why we're exhorted, "In his Presence is fullness of joy" (Psalm 16:11, NASB). Why would we ever stray from the abundance of joy available to us? Why do we settle for doing life without Presence?

Brené Brown might have given us part of the answer when she said, "When perfection is driving, shame is riding shotgun and fear is the annoying backseat driver."[36] Joy through Presence helps us lighten up and stop taking ourselves so seriously and removes the pressure of striving for perfection.

Presence lives in us, so by that very nature we are joy carriers! When we continue to cultivate life lived in the Presence of God, we understand that joy serves as a basis for Presence. Ultimately joy removes the need for external validation. In God's presence *is* the fullness of joy and the reality of love now and forevermore.

Perception Challenge and Exercise

Seeing yourself as a joy carrier immediately connects you to the Source of supply. You're not a downtrodden being. If you feel that way, it's simply an error in judgment. It's an illusion that can be shattered as soon as you identify the truth.

36   Brené Brown, interview by Oprah Winfrey, "Brené Brown: Perfectionism Is The 20-Ton Shield We Use To Protect Ourselves," *Huffington Post*, October 5, 2013, http://www.huffingtonpost.com/2013/10/05/brene-brown-perfectionism-shame-oprah_n_4045358.html.

Take a look: are you feeling the intoxicating bubbles of joy within you? If not, challenge your perspective. Welcome the truth of what you possess and what is available to you. You, my friend, are a joy carrier stocked and packed through and through. Awaken to your true identity!

Uprising! New Belief: You will never experience the sustaining fullness of joy without welcoming all parts of yourself home and becoming a safe place to dwell. And as you do, you will discover that you're the one that delayed attendance to the party because Love fully welcomed and accepted you long, long ago.

Maybe you're beginning to discover that the shifting of your limited perceptions will continue all of your days. Staying in sync with the Spirit will always provide amazing upgrades in your thinking that will continue to expand you into the fullness of love day to day. This is your portion, and this notion should elate you. What a phenomenal uprising!

Repeat out loud: I am a joy carrier and so there is never anything that need separate me from the Presence of Joy within me. I need not prove myself or strive for it; I need merely enter into it. Although life has challenges, life is joyful and to see it any other way is an illusion. I welcome the invitation to God, to joy and to life, which is the ultimate uprising!

DAY 42: UPRISING: YOU ARE THE PRIZE IN GOD'S CRACKER JACK

Sometimes I wonder if mental illness is not in part the wearing down of one's spirit and the repeated self-flagellating of the mind that doesn't know how to turn off. We have all sorts of good advice about rerouting information that fails to lead us back to the Source of wellbeing and River of life within us.

Francois Du Toit tells us, "We thought we must get revelation to drop from our head to our heart, but that's where we've had it wrong all along! It's the other way around; your heart knows much better than your head! It's from your innermost being that rivers flow... knowing with persuasion that you are God's idea; that you began in him and not in your mother's womb; realizing that Jesus didn't come as an example for you but of you; that Jesus is what the scriptures are all about, then you'll discover that you are what Jesus is all about."[37]

You're What It's All About

Study a small child wrapped up in his or her parent's adulation and you'll have a small inkling of God's thoughts towards us. Imagine being so alive to those constant loving thoughts. We learn how to love by being loved.

It's funny that often, when someone exhibits this kind of fully loved confidence, the tendency is to knock them down and teach them about humility

---

37   Francois Du Toit, Facebook post, February 10, 2014,
        https://www.facebook.com/francois.toit/posts/10151864215681216.

instead of embracing the perspective and reality they're living from. I sure want more shameless brazenness that allows me to grasp the reality that I am what God is all about! I want to believe it deeply in my bones so that I return fully to the young girl dancing in her tutu without thought or care. I want to be the one that runs ahead to skinny dip under a full moon because I live in the reality that I am free from shame.

If we are what God is all about, it pains him to see our self-flagellating posture. It pains him to see our lack of recognition of his life in us because he already took all the shame and doubt upon himself and buried it once and for all. We've received new wiring and clean-slate status in place of all our old stories. They've been washed away. All the non-lovers and resisters in our lives are immaterial when they appear before God's opinion of us. That's why we need to live life like we are loved.

All those labels stuck to our sides that are defiling us, even ones we've put upon ourselves, are heresy. The ignorance and hard-heartedness of spurned love that's stood to resist us, even our own, is only resisting what it can't comprehend; it's deluded and darkened in its understanding and ignorance. We are what the Creator thinks about every hour of every day. We are the hidden treasure that the parable speaks of, so valued that a man discovering it buried it again and purchased the land to own it (Matthew 13:44, NIV).

We previously discussed that the eye is the lamp. As Du Toit points out, "To walk in the light as He is in the light means to see your life and everything that concerns you, exclusively from your Father's point of view. You are indeed the focus of your Father's favor. To be convinced of your origin in God and the fact that God rescued His image and likeness in you in Christ is the vital energy of the law of liberty. To reflect... the opinion of

God, gives you radiance that makes your life irresistibly attractive!"[38]

There never was withholding nor will there ever be of this unfathomable Love, a Love so vast the ocean cannot contain it or the brightness of sunrise-to-sunset express it. Look around: nature trumpets this glorious "eye on the sparrow" care for all of creation. This sentiment is heralded in the Psalms: "How precious are your thoughts about me, O God. They cannot be numbered. I can't even count them; they outnumber the grains of sand! And when I wake up, you are still with me!" (Psalm 139:17–18, NLT). And again:

> You have examined my heart and know everything about me. You know when I sit down or stand up. You know my thoughts even when I am far away... You know what I am going to say even before I say it, Lord. You go before me and follow me. You place your hand of blessing on my head. Such knowledge is too wonderful for me, and too great for me to understand! I can never escape from your Spirit! I can never get away from your presence! (Psalm 139:1–2, 4–7, NLT)

Whenever we feel the struggle, the Creator already knows and has the perfect dose of medication we need wrapped up within his infilling and healing Love. He is telling us, as Hafiz did, "I wish I could show you when you are lonely or in darkness the astonishing light of your own being." Courage is loving ourselves for who we are and not who the world thinks we should be.

38   Francois Du Toit, Facebook post, March 6, 2017,
      https://www.facebook.com/francois.toit/posts/10154149657296216.

The Ultimate Youness!

Love is an absolute spiritual experience that makes us at home in our own skin, for it is the greatest appraisal we could receive. Awakening to being fully embraced, blessed and loved by God enables us to give ourselves the personal hospitality we so crave. All the things we use to describe ourselves and to base our identity on are swallowed up in the fact that our identity is purely based on the Love of God. This is the very definition of completeness that should make us giddy with joy.

"Love, joy, peace, patience, kindness, goodness, integrity, humility and self-control are not fragile, fading emotion, produced by willpower. They are the fruit of what you know in your spirit to be true about you. Fruit is the effortless, spontaneous expression of the character of the tree."[39] And that tree is the Tree of Life!

The *Mirror Bible* beautifully articulates Paul's words to the Galatians about this mystery: "So here I am dead and alive at the same time! I'm dead to the old me I was trying to be and alive to the real me which is Christ in me! Co-crucified, now co-alive! What a glorious entanglement! I was in him in his death; now he is in me in my life! For the first time I'm free to be me in my skin, immersed in his faith in our joint-sonship! He loves me and believes in me! He himself is his gift to me!" (Galatians 2:20, *Mirror Bible*).

Amazingly, the gift and invitation never expires and is articulated here again, plainly: "Behold, I stand at the door, and knock; if anyone hears my voice and opens the door, I will come in to him and will dine with him and

---

39   Francois Du Toit, Facebook post, February 4, 2017, https://www.facebook.com/francois.toit/posts/10154078213676216.

he with me" (Revelations 3:20, NASB).

Never is there a need to feel lonely. Never is there a need to feel an out-sider, separated and apart from the joy and acceptance of God, where we are fully embraced and intertwined in Love. We are invited to partake of good food, wine and relationship, not an impotent mental image. This available happiness has been gifted to us through the overflowing bounty, Presence and person of God! Welcome home!

Perception Challenge and Exercise

Paul exhorts us, "Regardless of what else you put on, wear love. It's your basic, all-purpose garment. Never be without it" (Colossians 3:14, MSG). Having love reside within you is the sweet fragrance and light of inner adornment that overflows from your life onto others. You don't create this light or stimulate it but merely recognize it. Challenge yourself to bathe in the River of delight and watch all manner of radiance shine forth. You are God's joy!

Uprising! New Belief: You have most likely spent your years seeking love and happiness in a slew of places when all along it was seeking you. There's no need to continue the search when you discover that happiness is alive and well and living inside you. It is a torrent of water and a blazing fire. It is all and everything you need.

Yes, you have to stoke the flame and stay close to the embers to feel the greatest warmth, but even when you fail to and it seems that it's all but died out, it hasn't. "By the waters of reflection my soul remembers who I am" (Psalm 23:3, *Mirror Bible*). Run in close, put your face on the breast of God and soak up the pulsing, vibrant heartbeat that calls your name. You are home, and it is here that you possess the happiness you've always wanted.

Embrace the ultimate happiness shift and discover this unrivaled transformation that at once causes a whole ocean of ferocious belief to be calmed and stilled. You can walk out onto the waters of life knowing that you are God's prize and at the same time have been given the greatest prize of all. Take it in and savor the intoxicating truth of this paradox. Hurdles and high jumps need no longer drive you. You are fully loved and embraced through and through.

Repeat out loud: I will feed my body, soul and spirit with the loving, life-affirming, benevolent and stupendous thoughts of God toward me. I will feast on being the treasure that was so valuable God gave it all to purchase me. I will keep myself in the current of God's affection as the ever-cleansing and renewing stream that it is. I will keep myself in the very present Love of God where true happiness is always within reach. I will own my me-ness and at-homeness in myself because I am the fully loved prize in God's box of Cracker Jack.

CONCLUSION

What a tremendous journey you have taken! Come back and revisit the path any time you want a new infusion. Spirit is alive and well and ready to guide you minute by minute. Listen for the knock at the door and be eager to open and receive new upgrades. I am thankful for the ever-expanding uprising in you! Go ahead, spread your wings and take flight! How can you fail? You're fully loved!

ABOUT THE AUTHOR

Artist and Professional Life Coach Kimber Britner leads women into the expanse of what's available with an untamed heart. For 25 years Kimber has worked with heart-centered individuals and groups of women, recognizing that many women know how to love everyone but themselves and struggle from a very real disconnection to their truest self. Unfortunately, it often takes a crisis to rock the boat and get women to recognize how deeply they've failed to love themselves, while working hard to "love their neighbor." Betraying one's innermost being is brutal on the body, soul and spirit and why it often shows up in poor health. Reconnecting women to the forgotten parts of themselves allows them to come alive in every way imaginable..

As an artist who paints and creates unique, one-of-kind jewelry, her main canvas is life design, where Kimber's authenticity and unique way of seeing things creates an atmosphere of transformation. Whether in her individual client work, workshops or retreats, she helps women see possibility, live from their own playbook and celebrate their lives. Kimber is a possibillionaire and she can't help but make other women excited about the possibilities too, but not before she helps them take an honest look at the systems their running that thwart the happiness they seek.

After being widowed at 36, Kimber tackled the daunting task of finding new inspiration in her life and raising four small children from the ages of two through nine on her own. Through the process, she became an expert in the art of innovation, repurposing her life and doing the hard work of learning to be present to what was going on within her. She taught herself a lifestyle of what she's coined as, "Personal Hospitality"; creating an inner climate of awareness, acceptance, non-judgment and loving care for oneself. She believes that you can hustle and drive yourself to no end, but if you haven't done the work of creating a welcoming inner climate, you won't enjoy the person you always come home to.

With a Certified Professional Coach (CPC) certification from the Institute of Professional Excellence in Coaching and an Associate Certified Coach (ACC) designation through the International Coaching Federation, as a Higher Ground Leadership® Certified Coach and a Certified Daring Way™ Facilitator (CDWF), which includes training in both The Daring Way™ and Rising Strong™ based on the pioneering research of Brené Brown, Kimber's keen intuition, depth of personal experience and coaching expertise help the women she works with thrive exponentially.

Kimber's first book, *Untamed Heart: Releasing Your Creative Genius*, is a fun, creative and lively road map for moving beyond your limitations into expansive possibilities.

Kimber is a great believer in thriving, a lover of life and enjoys spending it coaching clients, creating and hanging out with her husband, her brood of adult kids and newest addition, Winnie June.

To find Kimber's books, to inquire about coaching and schedule a free consultation, go to www.kimberbritner.com. Stay connected by signing up for Kimber's email list and receive the 7 days of Uprising Coaching in your inbox, free of charge.